Upcoast Summers

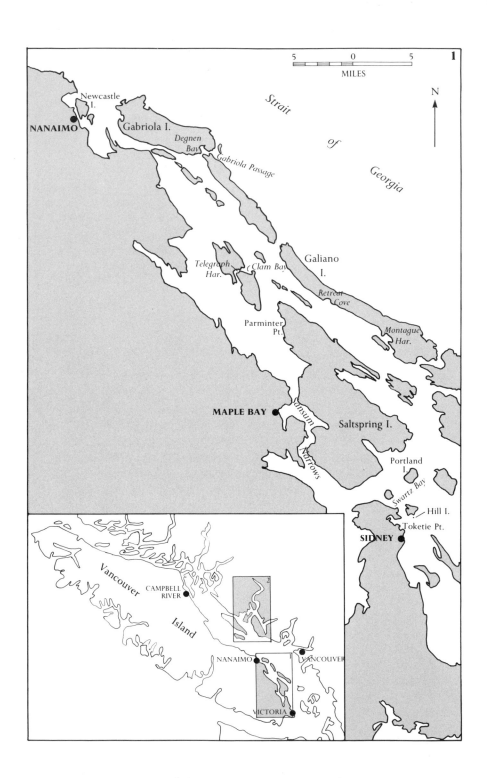

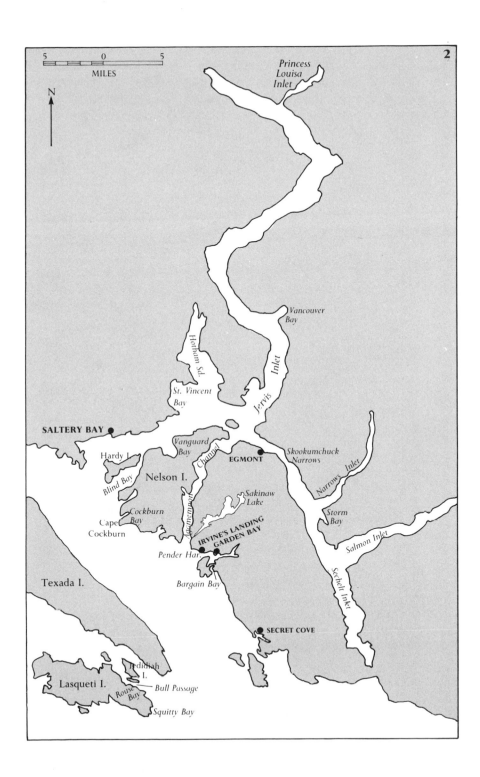

Princess
Louisa
Inlet

5   0   5
MILES

N

Vancouver
Bay

Hotham Sd.

*St. Vincent
Bay*

Jervis Inlet

SALTERY BAY ●

*Vanguard
Bay*

Hardy I.

Channel

EGMONT ●

*Skookumchuck
Narrows*

Narrows Inlet

Blind Bay

Nelson I.

*Sakinaw
Lake*

*Storm
Bay*

*Cockburn
Bay*

Cape
Cockburn

Agamemnon

**IRVINE'S LANDING
GARDEN BAY**

Pender Har.

Salmon Inlet

Bargain Bay

Texada I.

Sechelt Inlet

● **SECRET COVE**

*Jedidiah
I.*

Lasqueti I.

*Rouse
Bay*

— *Bull Passage*

Squitty Bay

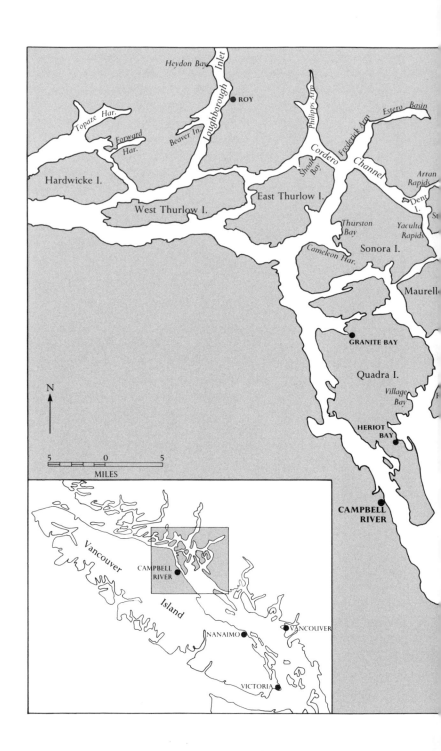

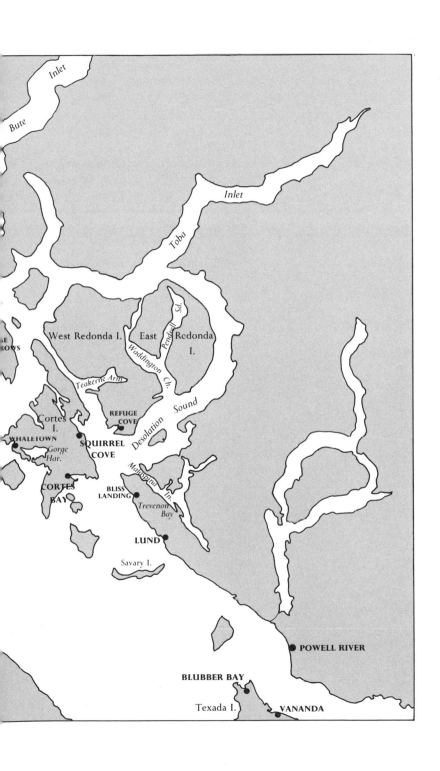

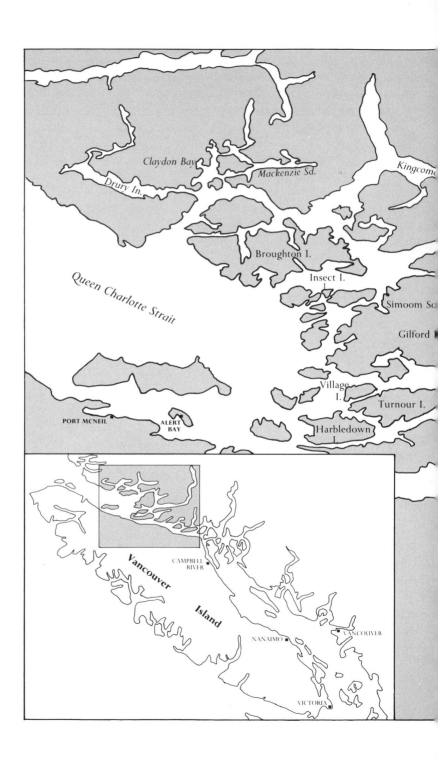

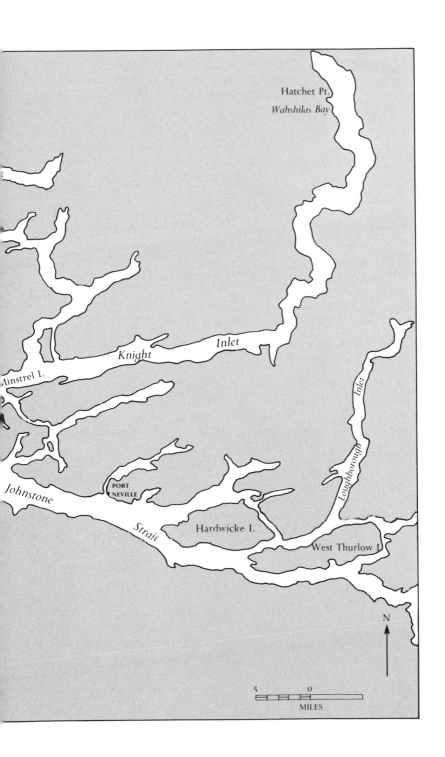

Upcoast Summers

by

Beth Hill

Horsdal & Schubart

Horsdal & Schubart Publishers Ltd.
Box 1
Ganges, B.C.
VOS 1E0

Cover painting by Jack Avison, Ganges, B.C.
Maps by Peggy Ward, North Vancouver, B.C.
Pictograph drawings by Dan Leen, Victoria, B.C.

Design and typesetting by The Typeworks, Vancouver, B.C.
This book is set in Perpetua.

Printed and bound in Canada by Hignell Printing Limited,
Winnipeg, Manitoba.

The search for information about the people in this book could be the preoccupation of a lifetime. Perhaps friends and descendants would like to send the publisher details which do not appear here, with the possibility that they would be included in a future edition.

Canadian Cataloguing in Publication Data

Barrow, Francis, 1876–1944
Upcoast Summers

Includes index.
ISBN 0-920663-01-X

I. Barrow, Francis, 1876–1944. 2. Pacific
Coast (Canada)–History. 3. Pacific Coast
(Canada)–Description and travel. I. Hill,
Beth, 1924- II. Title.

FC3817.3.B37 1985 971.1'303'0924 C85-090048-4 F1087.B37 1985

CONTENTS

PICTOGRAPHS

ACKNOWLEDGEMENTS

There would be no record of the *Toketie* summers if May John had not snatched some of the Barrow journals from a bonfire. May John, a descendant of the Saanich pioneer family named Michell, was married to Joseph John who had long worked for Amy and Francis Barrow and who was much loved by them. When Francis Barrow was dead and Amy in hospital, and their home was being emptied of their possessions, the cartons of papers were dumped onto a large fire. May John happened to arrive in time to save the documents used in the composition of this book. She is also re sponsible for finding an author to paste these fragments into a collage of coastal people and places. She has waited with great patience for this book, for she loved Francis and Amy Barrow like a daughter.

I am delighted to include here Dan Leen's accurate and sensitive drawings of some of the rock art which Francis and Amy Barrow recorded. The staffs of both the Provincial Archives of British Columbia and the National Museum have been helpful.

I am grateful to all the writers who have helped me to understand something of the British Columbia coast. *Raincoast Chronicles* and the writings of Gilean Douglas have been particularly enlightening. I have drawn facts from many sources, many of them listed at the back of this book.

My husband, Ray Hill, participated in the production of this book in many ways. He worked long hours in the darkroom to enlarge accurately the tiny photographs glued into the Barrow journals. He also piloted the 38-foot, buy-back fishboat, *Liza Jane*, in the track of the *Toketie*, 30 years after the Barrow summers. It has been difficult for me to refrain from inserting into this account my own very strong responses to the tide-scoured passages and places of the Inside Coast. The discipline in this regard was provided by the stern pencil of my editor, Maralyn Horsdal, gratefully acknowledged here.

INTRODUCTION

This book is an account of the travels of the little ship *Toketie*, bearing Francis and Amy Barrow and their black cocker spaniels, Rinnie and Nanette, on an exploration of the islands, inlets and harbours east of Vancouver Island, British Columbia, during the years from 1933 to 1941.

Poking into every bay and inlet, the Barrows shared the activities of the coastal people, giving Mr. Oien a hand with the haying, buying vegetables or dairy products from cash-short gardeners, inviting people for meals on the *Toketie* and going happily to dinner in log cabin, floating fish camp, logging camp, or wherever they were invited. "They insisted we stay for dinner" is a most common phrase in the Barrow journals. They picked berries, fished, had haircuts, did laundry on the beach, towed logs or boats, ferried people or things, helped sack charcoal, "yarned" with hundreds of lonely people, wrote letters for Phil Lavigne, played crib, helped set up Jim Stapleton's store—year after year they greeted old friends and new. The Barrows were coast dwellers themselves, not "tourists".

They also made a contribution of the utmost importance in the discovery and careful recording of Indian art on boulders or bedrock, both the petroglyphs (figures cut into the rock) and the pictographs (designs painted on the rock using red ochre or black soot, mixed with a bonding agent). The Provincial Archives in Victoria, B.C., and the National Museum in Ottawa preserve Barrow's work and his correspondence with two important friends, anthropologists William Newcombe and Harlan Smith, who encouraged and supported him. At Duck Bay on Salt Spring Island, for example, there are a few dull red marks on an area of eroding sandstone cliff, but only the most discerning archaeological eye would recognize that these once formed drawings in red ochre. In the days when the colour was brighter and the figures still visible, Francis and Amy Barrow visited the site to make a drawing and to take photographs. Without their work, this rock-art site, and many others, would have been lost.

According to her present owner, William Garden, the *Toketie* is the oldest operating yacht on the coast, has probably logged more miles than any other, and is now wearing out her sixth motor. Built for Francis Barrow at the Dafoe Machine Works in Vancouver soon after the turn of the century, in either 1903 or 1904, she was originally an open boat powered by a two-cylinder Lozier engine. By 1912, she had acquired a cabin and sometime after the First World War she was equipped with a two-cylinder Scripps engine. For the cruises of the Thirties described in this book she was propelled by a four-cylinder Universal gasoline screw engine. Considering the number of guests sometimes welcomed aboard, it is disconcerting to discover that the *Toketie* is only 26 feet in length and 7 feet 3 inches in width, with a depth of 3 feet 2 inches; her registered tonnage is 1.72. Although Barrow acquired the *Toketie* earlier, detailed summer sea journals survive for only 1933, 1934, 1935, 1936, 1938, 1939, 1940 and 1941. *Toketie* is said to mean "pretty" in the language of the Salish people of the Saanich Peninsula.

From the eight summers of adventuring, events have been selected to make one meandering route. As a consequence, incidents are not always in chronological order, but the reader may refer to the entry dates to explain any anomalies. The coast people of the Depression years are seen not only in the words of Francis Barrow's journal but also through the lens of his camera. All the photographs in the book are his. Unfortunately, the movies he made cannot now be found. Barrow's spelling of surnames has not been changed, and may not be accurate, but other obvious slips have been corrected.

Most of the coast dwellers whose names appear in the journals are not found in print elsewhere and only here and in the hearts of their descendants are they remembered. Perhaps the postmaster who enjoyed reading other peoples' letters is in this category. Others, like the Hallidays of Kingcome Inlet and Harry Roberts of Roberts Creek, are better known. That Barrow enjoyed and respected them all is obvious in his writing.

The sepia world of the Barrows is fading into the past and most of the people mentioned in this book are dead. Alive or dead, the individuals who happen to be recorded here are only a sample of those who lived on the Inside Coast in the Thirties. The Barrow journals and photographs bring this era to life again, and activities on the shores of the Strait of Georgia will be enriched by the presence of these ghosts.

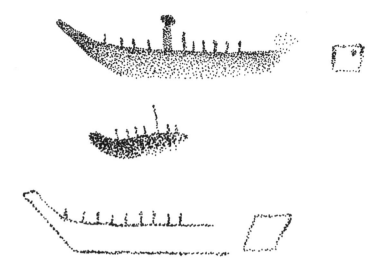

CHAPTER ONE

Wedged between Vancouver Island and the gigantic bulk of the continent of North America are hundreds of islands. In the long expanse of the Strait of Georgia they are widely dispersed, but north of 50° of latitude, they fit together like pieces of a jig-saw puzzle. Inlets probe deeply into the mountain ribs of the mainland. Twice a day, into these passages, straits and inlets thrusts a great surge of tide, crashing through rocky narrows in a maelstrom of white water. This land of islands, three hundred miles long, is here called the "Inside Coast", for it has no other collective name to reflect its unity.

The sunnier southern climate of the Strait of Georgia has always attracted settlers, but nowadays there seem to be more yachts than people among the islands at the northern end of the Inside Coast. Yachtsmen were rare in the Thirties. Instead, the waterways were everywhere busy with working boats – steamers, barges, tugs and log booms, fishboats of every size and design, gasboats, rowboats, canoes, sailboats, Indian dugouts, even houses on barges. These boats were used by the thousands of people who lived in the area — loggers, miners, prospectors, fishermen, recluses, storekeepers, farmers, Indians, trappers, hand-loggers, hand-liners, some retired folk, housewives, cooks, school teachers, children, nurses. But a half-century has brought changes. When the first easy harvest of the sea-edge timber was over, the forests came under the control of a few big logging companies, squeezing out the small operations; and when the big fishing companies monopolized the industry, canning fish only in Vancouver and Prince Rupert, they closed down all the small upcoast canneries. Then the life of the coast died. Its lifeline, the steamship service, ceased to operate.

So quickly does the raincoast forest reclaim its own that it seems sometimes as if these upcoast people never lived. However, during the Thirties they were observed and photographed by a middle-aged couple with two black dogs, who chugged along the watery roads in their small boat *Toketie*, "yarning" with everyone they met.

Who were the Barrows, whose words and pictures have preserved something of our coastal past? Born in 1876, at West Hill, Putney, in London, Francis Barrow was the third surviving child of Sarah Constance Mallet and Alexander Maclean Barrow. "He was always delicate and lived with his mother at Holygrove, Fittlesworth, in Sussex," his niece Bonella Woodhead has written.[1] She also remembers that Francis went to school at Lancing, studied mining in Cornwall, and served as a private in the First World War. He was fond of practical jokes and loved playing with children. He could make fine kites and built a large-scale toy railroad for his nephew and nieces, and a charming dollhouse. On this coast, he performs tricks to amuse Brown Horth's children on a rainy day in Teakerne Arm. The Barrows had no children of their own.

Recording her childhood memories, his mother, Sarah Mallet, born in 1839, described her Dublin home.[2] She wrote of the visit of Queen Victoria to Ireland in 1849, of her dear sister Jenny dying of cholera in the Fort of Allahabad during the Indian Mutiny, and of her brother Willie, a professor in Tuscaloosa, Alabama, when the American Civil War broke out. As Sarah Mallet also came to visit her son Francis at North Saanich, British Columbia, her reminiscences seem to bring the past close to the present, in a world-wide network.

Amy Bradford was one of the many daughters of Sir John and Lady Bradford. Brought up in a magnificent home at Haywards Heath, Sussex, she graduated from the Munich Conservatory of Music in Germany and was an excellent swimmer, tennis player and horsewoman. It seems a long step from such a life to the *Toketie* summers, when Amy would make apple jelly for old Ned Breeze of Cortes Island.

Because of a chest "delicacy" (associated, perhaps with a slightly malformed shoulder) Francis Barrow was sent in 1903 to visit his older brother Arthur, a land surveyor in British Columbia. On a week-long rowing holiday with Arthur among the Gulf Islands, Barrow packed in his duffle bag a cardboard-covered Scribbling Diary. The diary gives a tantalizingly brief glimpse of this experience which changed his life. April can be a halcyon month in the Strait of Georgia. Although he returned to England in November, he was back in British Columbia in 1905; he settled on a small island near Sidney, where he struggled to produce chickens and eggs. It was not until September 20, 1906, that Amy and Francis were married, returning to honeymoon on Saturna Island, then moving into a home near Sidney. Like many of the expatriate English people of British Columbia history, the Barrows were supported by incomes from "home": in the Barrows' case by Amy Barrow's fortune. This permitted them to enjoy a hobby-farming life in North Saanich and long and leisurely summers at sea.

When the warm winds of early summer began to blow, the Barrows would set off. No two departures are the same. One year Barrow wrote:

> We were busy all day cleaning up and putting things away. In the afternoon I brought *Toketie* to the float, it being too low tide in the morning. There was a fresh easterly wind with whitecaps over the bay which made loading difficult and Amy had a nasty fall into the boat, bruising herself painfully and spilling the cakes. However, at 5.30 P.M. we got started and went over to say good-bye to the Payne families at Saturna, but found them all away. We went on to Hugh's where we had supper on board. We got gas and several things and Don came down to tighten the reverse gear.

Departure meant a meandering trip north to Nanaimo, saying good-bye to friends en route. Rarely did they pass Telegraph Harbour on Thetis Island without a visit with the Sidney Booths. Timing their passage through Dodd Narrows to run with the tide, they tied up at Anderson's Boat House in Nanaimo Harbour, where the mechanic frequently did last-minute repairs. Always the last goodbye was from their friend Tom Higgs. Within the sheltering islands of Nanaimo Harbour they would linger, waiting for favourable winds in the wide Strait of Georgia, sometimes poking the *Toketie* into the strait at dawn, just to see "if the Gulf was kind" and returning to shelter if it was not. The best crossings were made early in the morning, when the sea was opalescent and the winds were asleep, when the prow of slow-moving *Toketie* would slit the smooth surface like a knife, leaving a ragged wake unravelling behind.

CHAPTER TWO

We left Nanaimo at 5.35 A.M. and there was a black cloud-bank to the S.W. All went well, and as we approached Lasqueti Id. the wind freshened and we were glad to turn into Bull Passage as the waves were somewhat big, with whitecaps. While we descended one wave, the canoe was mounting one astern, but she shipped no sea. We are now, at 8.15 A.M. anchored in the snug little bay on Jedediah Id. where Capt. Anderson and I landed in 1934. We are enjoying that experience, which all people who travel around in boats must appreciate, of lying in a safe quiet anchorage and listening to the wind howling outside.

(July 2, 1936)

In the evening it cleared a bit and we rowed round to an even better bay near the N.W. end of Jedidiah Id. and opposite a small unnamed island, a narrow channel separating them. We

took the water-tank and a bucket along and found a fine water
hole on the beach, fed by a small spring. I suspected there
might be something of this sort as I noticed a hand-logger working here in 1934.

(July 3, 1936)

Rowing near Jedidiah Island,
    I turned the flashlight on the water and saw countless thou-
sands of dogfish swimming about the boat. As far as one flashed
the light one could see shining eyes. I have never seen so many
dogfish in my life.

(September 4, 1939)

We ran to the fish-buyer's floating store in Rouses' Bay, Lasqueti Id. We talked to one of the trollers. He suggested towing
the canoe from the waterline, which good hint I carried out
and found she came along fine. Late last evening a troller came
into the bay and anchored close by. This morning we made his
acquaintance and found he was Mr. George Sweet, who owns
the island in Bull Passage next to Jedediah Id. He says it is
named Bull Id. Soon after 1 P.M. Sweet and I walked along the
trail which was overhung with bracken and pretty wet, and
called on Mr. and Mrs. Hughes. They gave us tea, and after a
pleasant chat I returned to *Toketie*. Amy had got a tommy-cod
while I was away and now she has just gone off to catch
another. I see the glass is going up steadily so there is a chance
of finer weather to follow.

(July 4, 1936)

George Sweet and his lifelong friendly rival, Jimmy Riddell, were
two of the best fishermen in the area. Once, when the fishing was
not too good and Jimmy had been trolling without much success
during most of a long day, he saw George Sweet's boat approaching. Quickly he rehooked his entire catch, planning to pull them in
conspicuously just as the *Bridgwater* slid past. But when the line
came in, it had only fish heads on it, a seal having devoured the rest.
    A veteran of the Boer War, George Sweet named his troller after
his English birthplace. At first he lived aboard the *Bridgwater* but in
1910 he pre-empted Bull Island and built the log cabin he occupied
until he was too old to live alone on an island. Jimmy and George
were leaders in the fishermen's cooperative movement and some of
the important early meetings were held at Rouses' Bay.

As we were nearing Squitty Bay [Lasqueti Island] we met the *Solander,* Bill waving a pair of overalls to attract our attention. They had lost eight sections of a boom they were towing a couple of days ago, and the logs were scattered along the Lasqueti Id. shore. Bill had the local fishermen out collecting logs. He came aboard and had a yarn. We then went into Squitty Bay and tied up at the float. We visited Mr. and Mrs. White, whose son we met at Nanaimo two years ago. They came down to *Toketie* and we had games of three-handed crib, but it was not my lucky day.

(September 4, 1936)

At the N.W. end of Jedidiah Id. we walked up to see Mr. and Mrs. Hughes and they insisted on us staying to lunch, which we had under the trees in the orchard. Their fisherman friend Riddell and their boarder were there too.

(July 7, 1938)

This pear orchard, and the sweetness of the pears, is well remembered by oldtimers on Lasqueti Island. In those Depression years the price received for produce shipped to Vancouver was sometimes so low that it did not pay the freight costs. At that time the Hughes sold their pears to their neighbours on Lasqueti, one dollar for a 40 pound box, pears without blemish, sweet and juicy. Some years after the Barrow visit, when both Jennie Hughes' husband and Jimmy Riddell's wife were dead, Jimmy and Jennie were married, sharing their retirement years at Pender Harbour.

Many of the islanders whom the Barrows visited were almost without money. "We couldn't mail a letter for two years," remarked Bessie Dane, a long-time coast resident.[1] On Lasqueti Island, the road foreman was also the relief officer, trying to allot the work so that all might have enough to eat. A man with a wife and eight dependent children received $27 per month; to get this money, he had to declare himself "indigent", a humiliating and hated word. Single women could not work on the roads or go to a relief camp, or even be claimed as dependents if they were over 21. Some young women fished in rowboats, others gardened, attempting to support themselves. Servant or waitressing work hardly existed. Of course everyone grew food, preserving it in root cellars and glass sealers. They ate wild fruit, clams, venison and fish. It was illegal to have bottled venison, even during those hard years, but landowners could get a "Farmer's Licence" to kill one deer per month. As the Depression wore on, the deer on some islands became scarce indeed. However, in spite of shortages, the coastal people were generous and hospitable, ready to share whatever they had, as the Barrows discovered, wherever they went.

> In the morning Amy and I johnsoned [i.e. motored. The *Toketie* had a Johnson outboard motor used on the dinghy.] round to our old anchorage to get water and disturbed a big old 'coon digging clams on the sand flat. Amy found a slate knife.
>
> (July 9, 1938)

The slate knife is an Indian artifact, one of many which the Barrows collected; they were later given to the British Columbia Provincial Museum.

> We went over on our return to have a yarn with the people on the tug *Totem*, Capt. Allen. He came in at 3 A.M. with a tow of poles and was pleased to get shelter. At 4 P.M., the wind having died down a lot, we pulled out. There was a swell, but no breaking seas.
>
> (July 9, 1938)

From Lasqueti Island it is a short run east to Secret Cove, a snug harbour on the mainland, sheltered by Thormanby Island. Here the Barrows called on Mrs. Larsen and Mr. Bryndlesohn.

> Fisherman's Cove. We arrived about 11.30 and now at noon Amy is producing the swellest kind of smells from the cooking department: beef-steak and tomatoes. The dogs are chewing bones and everyone is happy, so who would worry if it is raining in torrents. We got a letter from Woods, Armitage's partner. He said one of their neighbours went out hunting deer and never came back. They had searched for him in vain. A little while ago one of the Hanson boys and another fisherman were anchored at Channel Id. when a grizzly bear came swimming straight for their boat and they had to shoot it to keep it from climbing aboard. This Hanson boy saw a sea-serpent in Pryce Channel some time ago, but this time he had the bear to show.
>
> (September 13, 1939)

> We made fast to Mrs. Larson's float. Amy cooked the ham as we came along. We got some home-made bread which Mrs. Lar-

son had baked yesterday and some potatoes. Also some home-made strawberry jam, but I don't think it is as good as her bread.

(September 14, 1939)

It was a very windy day. Two boats came in for shelter and made fast to the government float, and the tug *Belle* had a boom inside the cove. We walked along a trail to the north outlet of the cove and looked across to Texada. One could get out of the cove here in a row-boat, but the channel is too rocky for motor craft. We rowed over and had a chat with Mr. Bryndlesohn.

(September 15, 1939)

Stocked up at the store as provisions were running low. After lunch we went across the cove to the government float and made fast. It is a very well-built affair, with shed and fixings, but it is very little used. We walked up to the celebrated road which joins Gibson's Landing and Pender Harbour, on which was spent very many thousands of dollars. There is much rock work. We walked on and on in the direction of Half Moon Bay but never met a soul, nor did we see any house. As we got on the road a car came by, the only car we saw in a walk which lasted several hours. Perhaps it was the only car between Pender Harbour and Gibson's Landing.

(September 16, 1939)

The Sunshine Coast Highway connecting Pender Harbour and Gibson's Landing, started in the early Thirties, was built by an army of the unemployed. Pushed through by 1936, the road was unpaved until about 1950. Bessie Dane remembered that the men who worked on the road lived in a camp where Madeira Park is now, and that they were paid two dollars per day for their labour. At that time, such a wage seemed very high to the local people.

We went to see Mr. Bryndlesohn and saw his garden which is always nice. Mr. Bryndlesohn visited us later on. After tea Amy and I went for a walk along the Pender Harbour-Gibson's Landing road, about three inches thick in dust, but as usual no car or pedestrians; but on our way down to the boat we heard a car in the distance, which was something.

(July 19, 1941)

We spent the day scraping grease and getting all the water out of the bilge, after which I doused every compartment with creoline, which I then mopped out with a rag. The foul smell which we have endured for some time is much better. It was handy being opposite the wharf shed in which I put the stove and other things while cleaning the bilge. We went over to the store in the evening to get a few things, and Mrs. Larson gave us a rubbed slate spear head not quite complete. Mrs. Larson is baking bread for us.

(July 20, 1941)

We moved across to Mrs. Larson's float and after lunch we got our three loaves of bread. At 12.45 P.M. we left for Garden Bay and made fast to the store float here after a run of an hour and twenty-five minutes. We walked along the lake trail to the Mitchell's and at the far end of the lake found a bulldozer and compressed air outfit at work, a road being put into Garden Bay. They are shooting 65 holes tomorrow. We found Mrs. Mitchell at home, but Mr. Mitchell was at the store at Pender Harbour to see his daughter who was not well. Mr. Green, brother of the Rev. Allan Green of the Columbia Coast Mission called. He is also a parson. Mrs. Mitchell gave us all tea, and shortly after Mr. Green, Amy and I walked back to Garden Bay, meeting Mr. Mitchell before we struck the trail to the lake. Mr. Green knew Arthur [Barrow] when he was at Smithers. On getting back to *Toketie*, Mr. Green came on board and had a drink of grapefruit juice. Drs. Wray, Johnston and Simpson came on the float and Dr. Johnston visited us a little while and had a chat and a grapefruit juice. Since there are so many boats tied up to the floats, we moved on up the harbour and made fast to the government float in Klein's Bay, which we had to ourselves, and where we spent a very comfortable night. We were here last year when Brown Horth and his family were here. It is a nice spot.

(July 21, 1941)

Pender Harbour at the time of the Barrows' visits was still a closely-knit water community, consisting of the large main concourse with inlets and passages branching off. The Williams Island light still blinks at the western entrance. On the port side as the *Toketie* entered was Irvine's Landing, where the first known non-Indian settler, Chinaman Harry, probably built a cannery. It was later sold to Henry Irvine who in turn sold to Portuguese Joe Gonsalves, the owner when the Barrows arrived. Across the harbour entrance is the government dock at a place called Pope's Landing, still owned by Mr. Pope in the Thirties. About one mile into the harbour, on the north side, stands St. Mary's Hospital. Beyond Garden Bay to the east, the harbour narrows and through this neck lies Gunboat Bay, the territory of the Kleins. Whiskey Slough to the south was named for the Saturday night parties of the Scottish gill-netters. Brought to the coast to operate a herring saltery, the Scots became gillnetters, disliked by the seine men and the hand-line fishermen because they "caught too damn many fish", in the days when gillnetting was virtually unrestricted.[2] The Saturday night parties aboard the fishboats were their substitute for the friendly pubs of the grey-stone Scottish villages so far away.

A boat was at the float when we woke up, and presently Mr. Will Klein and another Klein who we met at their logging camp at Okosollo Channel several years ago, rowed up to the float and went on board. Mr. Will Klein is going to make his oysters perform for my movie camera tomorrow. After supper we rowed up to the head of the harbour and landed at Mr. Frederick Klein's place. We got some water and vegetables and he showed us his collection of Indian implements which he had found on the place. He had some nice rubbed slate points and among other things a concretion scraper carved on each side. On another concretion, a carved face. I do not think we have met Mr. Frederick Klein before, but there are six families of Kleins living in this part of the harbour and it takes time to sort them out.

(July 23, 1941)

The three Klein brothers, Bill, Charles and Fred, established a logging camp of about 30 men at Pender Harbour in 1912, and among the trees they cut are the famous giants forming Lumberman's Arch in Vancouver's Stanley Park. All the Kleins, untypical loggers, stayed to clear land, dyke the saltmarshes and settle permanently at the eastern end of Pender Harbour, naming their area Kleindale. After Fred had established his homestead, planted peach, plum and apple orchards, married and had children, he found time to prospect for gold seven miles back in the mountains to the east. He also started the oyster beds of Kleindale. When the

British Columbia writer Will Dawson met Fred Klein at his old Gunboat Bay farm in 1955, he described Fred as a very tall man, powerful and strong, with a large nose and a firm chin. When Will asked Fred what was the world's chief trouble, Fred thought for a moment before he spoke: "Mostly too many middle-men—fellers trying to get a fat living without working. I don't like them. I bought a team once. They looked good, a good match. I shot one. It lay back in the traces, let the other do all the work."[3]

> In the morning I went up to the oyster beds which were uncovered and I took some shots of Will Klein of the Pender Harbour Oyster Co., gathering some oysters which he put on one of the floats. Later I took shots of him opening oysters. In the afternoon Harry Barnes and a Major from Victoria with him visited us. Soon after 5 o'clock I rowed up to the oyster beds where W. Klein had put some on one of the floats, the oysters being about to spawn so that it would spread among the other oysters on the float, thereby stimulating them so as to induce them to spawn. I was ready with the movie camera to take this unique shot. Klein said he was sure a movie of this process had not been taken. One oyster spawned in a half-hearted manner and we waited till it got too dark to shoot film without any further action among the oysters. Klein says when the oysters spawn they pump the spawn in a milky flow for about ten minutes, and this is carried from one end of the float to the other and then away by the tide, the water in the float being so white that you cannot see the oysters. They usually spawn at high tide and the warmth of the water has something to do with it, a hot day being more favourable than a cold one. However, notwithstanding the stimulation, Klein said one could not be sure of causing the oysters to spawn, although he was usually successful.
>
> (July 24, 1941)
>
> After lunch at Portugee Joe's Hotel, we said goodby to Portugee Joe and his partner Theo Dames and went over to Pope's Store and Amy got some shoes which she has needed, her toes sticking out of the ones she had.
>
> (September 12, 1934)

It is said that Portuguese Joe Gonsalves left his Madeira Islands home while still a young boy, working on sailing ships. He is supposed to have arrived in Gastown at the age of 17, in 1874. By 1904 he had saved enough money to buy the Irvine's Landing store and hotel, in partnership with a short, stocky Latvian named Theodore Dames, who became his son-in-law. Local history records a third newcomer at this time, Joe Perry from Cape Verde, a giant of a man, almost black in colour. Perry was well liked by the other settlers at Pender Harbour, and historian Jackie Holecka writes that the children loved to listen to his tales of tropical ports and oceans. Joe Perry was not only the skipper of Joe Gonsalves' seine boat, the *Hermosa,* but also the gardener and the bouncer in the saloon. Theo Dames, a great lover of books and classical music, came originally from Riga on the Baltic Sea. His wife was an important figure in Pender Harbour life. According to Holecka, the Pender Harbour baseball games and dances of those days were like large family picnics over which Mrs. Dames presided like a benevolent aunt. She knew everyone because everyone did their shopping at the Landing on steamer days.

> We went through the narrows to the head of the harbour and got eggs and milk from Mr. Loughlin. His relations who have the Indian carved stone dog are not logging at Bargain Harbour, so we did not see it. After supper we rowed up to the oyster beds and saw Mrs. Klein and got a bottle of cream from her.
>
> (June 29, 1935)

> Soon after 3 P.M. we started off to walk to Sakinaw Lake. I enquired the way from Mr. Drummond Wolfe who lives about half way along the trail. I went on ahead of Amy, who kept pace with old Nanny. Mrs. Wallace was at home and I had a chat with her until Amy and Nanny arrived. Amy and I then went across the lake about 200 yards away and we found the very interesting groups of pictographs. On our return across the lake, we met Mr. Wallace and he and I had a chat about Indian things. He refused to take payment for the hire of the boat, though that is his business and we left at 7.45 for Pender Harbour. Nanny came along like a two-year-old.
>
> (July 1, 1935)

Bessie Dane spoke of "my old friend Mr. Wolfe." She said he was a very well-educated Englishman who told her that he had come to Pender Harbour because he was tired of people always standing behind his chair, referring to the servants of his English home. Although he apparently wanted to be free of the social conventions of his English life, "he never let himself go like so many of the old country people did".[4]

We had herrings for lunch as well as breakfast, which Henry Whitaker got last night and which he had cleaned for us. About 2 P.M. we johnsoned round to the White House [the Whitaker home] and took photos of it and the Whitakers. We then went through the canal into Bargain Harbour and called on Schouler who was with the I.W.T. during the war. He was reported dead, and when he got home he found his wife had married again. We then went to see the Potts who had Mrs. Potts' mother, Mrs. Burnette, staying with them, and several other people. They showed us their very fine collections of old South Sea weapons and curios.

(September 7, 1935)

We were greeted by Gonzales, Mrs. Dames, Bill and later on by the Whitaker family and Mr. Potts the postmaster. Mrs. Dames insisted we should have tea 'on the house' and it was nice to find such friendship. We moved round to our old berth by the gas tank and Mr. Whitaker came on board for a chat and to tell us all the news. We miss old Frenchy Fontaine, who used to carry mail and passengers up the inlet. He got into trouble for not carrying sufficient life-saving apparatus and has now gone to live near Vancouver, running a chicken farm. He married the cook at Gonzales Hotel last year. It looks like rain tonight. The *Lady Pam* arrived just before dusk and there was the usual gathering of local inhabitants on the dock. After discharging a lot of freight, the *Lady Pam* left for the head of Jervis Inlet.

(July 9, 1938)

The world smelt very pleasant after the rain. We rowed through the canal and visited Mr. Schouler who has had a stroke some time ago. We were pleased to find that he had regained the use of his arm and leg but they are still far from normal. Schouler showed us a few Indian things he had found in the garden. He said he had sold most of the things he had found to a man in Nanaimo who had passed them on to the Smithsonian Institute.

(July 10, 1938)

We then went up to the Hospital wharf and I saw about getting the battery charged at the hospital. The orderly came down and took the two batteries up in the hospital truck and we took them to the charging room. After lunch I went ashore close by where we anchored and set up the camera to take a movie of the hospital when Dr. Johnson arrived, as he thought I was a surveyor. We talked about movie cameras (Dr. J. has one), archaeology and other subjects till the doctor suggested I had better shoot my film as it was very hot and I might blister the film in the camera. He did this when he and his wife were in Arizona. At 4.30 I went up to the hospital and took movies of the staff, and before returning to *Toketie* visited R. McKichan, the Saanichton doctor on the *John Antle*. He is quite anxious to get home as nobody is looking after his practice, but they seem slow in sending up relief. In the evening I went up to the hospital again and Dr. Johnson showed me the Chapel and all over the Hospital and then film of his honeymoon trip from Manitoba to Arizona and California. The sunset as viewed from the hospital was glorious, the mouth of Pender Harbour and Texada Island in the distance.

(August 6, 1940)

In the morning we went over from our anchorage to the wharf and Wally Smith took us over the *John Antle*. She seems a very suitable boat for these waters, but Wally Smith says she has not enough engine power. She used to be a seiner. We then walked along the trail by the lake and arrived after half an hour at the Mitchells. They insisted on us staying to lunch. We arrived back shortly before 3 P.M. and the hospital orderly brought down the batteries to the wharf. We had supper at the cafe in Garden Bay. I am writing this by electric light and have put the gas lamp away.

(August 7, 1940)

The union of the gas line I found to be leaking and on tightening it up I broke the soldered joint on the nipple. The orderly at the hospital phoned to the various stores to see if they had a ⅛th union but we had no luck, so we rowed to Dusenbury's. He told us his brother in Bodega Anchorage died some little while ago. I started to take out part of the fuel line. Later on I got the joint soldered, and shellaced the union, and got the engine started about 3.30 P.M.

(August 8, 1940)

Harry Dusenbury was a boat builder who had set up shop on an island in Whiskey Slough. When the Scottish fishermen gathered there on Saturday nights, Harry's twanging fiddle was the life of the parties. He was also a prime mover and a hard worker in the establishment of St. Mary's Hospital at Pender Harbour.

The story of the hospital began long before the happy day in 1930 when it opened for service. The hospital was paid for by public subscription, and the excavation and all preliminary work were done by the people of Pender Harbour, but the man primarily responsible for its existence was John Antle. Born in Newfoundland, Antle had his Master Mariner's papers even before his ordination in the Anglican Church. Sailing from Vancouver to Alert Bay with his son, in a 14-foot boat, he recognized the absence of medical or religious services for the people of the Inside Coast. He talked the Anglican Synod into starting the Columbia Coast Mission in 1904 and a year later he opened the Queen's Hospital at Rock Bay on Vancouver Island (later St. Michael's Hospital) and launched the hospital ship *Columbia*. It was estimated that the mission would serve 3,000 men in 84 logging and mining camps, as well as hundreds of small settlements and the Indian villages. A second hospital, St. George's, was opened at Alert Bay in 1909, the Kwakiutl people contributing $1,400 to pay for the X-ray unit. The next step was the conversion of a dance hall on log floats at Texada Island to serve as the Columbia Hospital. When the Texada copper mines were abandoned, the hospital was floated to O'Brien Bay in Knight Inlet. (To this hospital John Antle once towed a house on floats because the sick mother had no one with whom to leave four small children.) Later, this moveable hospital was being towed to Pender Harbour when a gale in Johnstone Strait piled it on the rocks. Determined to have a hospital, the people of Pender Harbour built St. Mary's.

John Antle was both skipper and minister. He knew what was involved in carrying a sick person over iced logs, on a door hastily torn from a shack. Once when he was conducting a service in the chapel of the *Columbia,* a man shouted from the shore that there had been a bad accident in a camp up Johnstone Strait. Antle slammed closed the Bible, pulled off his surplice, started the motor, cast off and headed out. One of the abandoned worshippers, hastily leaping ashore, remarked, "That was the best sermon I ever heard!"[5]

In 1936 John Antle, aged 71, decided to retire. At 75 he crossed the Atlantic in the 40-foot yawl *Reverie*, avoiding German mine fields, and experiencing terrible gales which shredded the sails. On a wet and windy day in November 1949, he died of a heart attack aboard the *Reverie*, then tied up at Vancouver.

The good friend who had long worked with John Antle, and who inherited the command of the Columbia Coast Mission, was the Reverend Alan D. Greene, whose brother encountered Francis Barrow on the trail to Garden Bay Lake. Greene loved to tell the story of the logger who was so anti-religious that he refused to even acknowledge Greene's smile. However, Greene persisted in his friendliness for 30 years and one day, suddenly, the logger thrust out his hand: "You win, Reverend, I can't stay mad any longer."[6]

The first matron at St. Mary's Hospital was Bessie Dane. "Boy, we had fun!" she said. However, there were many times during the Thirties when Mrs. Bradly, the hospital cook, would tell Bessie there was nothing to eat. Then Bessie would set off in the rowboat, sometimes to catch a fish, sometimes to find a fisherman, or to ask the neighbours for food. The Mitchells were always generous. "Oh, the Mitchells of Pender Harbour!" Bessie has said. "They were wonderful people."[7]

> We went on to Irvine's Landing where we had lunch and filled up with gas, coal oil and stores. We sent off various books which had been lent us on our cruise, and the manuscript of Francis Dickie's "Tomorrow's Journeyings." After a yarn with Mr. Potts, we ran up the harbour to the island near the hospital and called on Captain and Mrs. Jermain.
>
> (September 12, 1941)

> After lunch, which included some New Zealand spinach which Captain Jermain gave us and which was very good, the sun came out and the day very much improved. We ran to Irvine's Landing where we met Mr. and Mrs. Mackenzie. Mr. Mackenzie used to have a butcher's shop at the end of the hotel but found it did not pay and so went handlogging. He lost his foot

in an accident three months ago and is going about on crut-
ches. At 2.45 the weather was so fine we went on.

(September 14, 1941)

Leaving all their Pender Harbour friends, the Barrows passed the
Williams Island light and turned *Toketie's* prow northwards. Only a
short run to the north, two narrow inlets slice into Nelson Island:
Cockburn Bay and Billings Bay. Locally, Cockburn Bay has been
known as Chack-Chack Bay, after the famous sailboat built there.
The builder of the *Chack-Chack*, Harry Roberts, was the next coast
dweller to welcome the Barrows.

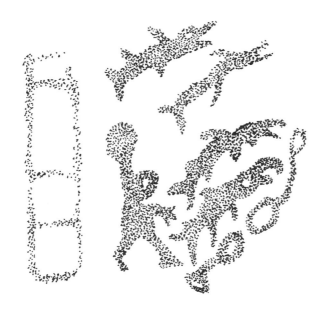

CHAPTER THREE

Billings Bay. As it was low water we anchored outside the narrow entrance and I went through to look for rocks. We went through all right and made fast to Roberts' float. We had a very friendly greeting from the Roberts family and were taken over their delightful log house which is unique in its way. I think they must have had much pleasure in building it and it is quite out of the common run of formal rooms.

(September 13, 1939)

"Unique" and "quite out of the common run" are apt descriptions for almost everything associated with Harry Roberts. In 1900, young Harry celebrated his sixteenth birthday on the glorious day he arrived in Vancouver from England. Unable to contain his eagerness, he only stayed overnight in the city, and then set out to paddle a 16-foot canoe to the land now named Roberts' Creek, which his uncle had pre-empted. Two days later the keel of his boat grated on the land to which he was to devote his passion, energy and intelligence. Arriving as a greenhorn, he quickly learned the skills of the homesteader, working with his father, Frank, and his uncle, Dan Steinbrunner. By 1904 he had purchased 40 acres from his father, earning money by working with Hubert Whitaker of Sechelt on the steam tug *Hubert,* towing logs and scows in Sechelt Inlet. He built a house on his land before he married Effie "Birdie" Sisson in 1905. By 1907 he had built the first store at the mouth of Roberts Creek, opening for business with $40 invested in a stock which included bacon coated with gelatin (to keep it from mildew), cheese in circular wooden boxes, sacks of flour and sugar, two-gallon jars of strawberry and lemon drops, MacDonalds Best tobacco and little bags of Bull Durham, and of course Dodd's Kidney Pills.

In 1910 he took over the job of postmaster. The mail was brought up the coast about once a week by the *S.S.Comox* of the Union Steamship Company. As there was no wharf, the steamship would whistle for Harry to row out, a pleasant task on a calm summer day but perilous in a 20-knot southeaster. On stormy days the ship's crew, with exquisite timing, would toss the mail bag into the skiff as steamer and tiny rowboat crested a wave side by side. When the skiff was rowed to shore, Harry would jump overboard into the icy shallows to guide the boat up the beach as each succeeding wave pushed it. Four years later Harry had convinced the government that a dock should be constructed, and the timbers for the wharf probably came from the sawmill he had opened in 1910. On the bright red face of the first freight shed on the new wharf, he painted the words SUNSHINE BELT in large white letters.

The house that the Barrows visited was called "Sunray". At first Harry called it "The House of 10,000 Faces" because it had more than 300 pieces of glass in its unusual windows, which were designed to look like large spider webs. The light danced and flashed from the panes. It was a low-slung log house with 20 sides, set in a garden of bright flowers. Inside the front door, steps descended into an amphitheatre with a cement floor painted to look like a stained glass window. Around the walls were enough bunks to sleep a dozen people. All the furniture, and the house itself, came from trees growing nearby, shaped by Harry's hand. "I've done everything myself," he remarked. "I'm a single hander."[1]

I took a film of *Toketie* and *Leo* lying at the float, and shortly after Cherry [Harry Roberts' second wife] and the baby arrived. Some time after we all walked back to the house, but near the pump-house Amy had the misfortune to slip on the dry grass and put her ankle out. She suffered much pain, but stuck it out in her usual plucky manner. She lay there, and we did what we could, Roberts bathing her foot with cold sea water which after a time eased the pain a bit, and we were able to get Amy to the house. We stayed there all day. In the evening Harry Roberts got some sea weed which he heated up and packed around Amy's foot, and she said it eased the pain.

(July 26, 1941)

Amy's foot was a little better when I went up to the house about 10 o'clock. We had dinner with the Roberts, and after tea on the beach we got Amy into the boat and left for Blind Bay, and made fast to the float.

(July 27, 1941)

Northward again went the *Toketie,* into the salty sea wind, with the coastal strip of rocks and jagged trees sliding southward on the starboard side, a further strip of mountain peaks behind, moving more slowly. The Barrows were headed for Hardy Island, to visit Mr. Macomber and Tom Brazil.

Arrived Blind Bay after lunch, a stew. Custard and stewed prunes. We tied up at Mr. Macumber's float, no boats being there for a wonder. Mr. Macumber had left shortly before on his motor yacht *Principia* for Princess Louise Inlet. Tom Brazil came in soon after we had tied up. He had been out to meet the Union boat and put on mail. Tom gave me a piece of T. & B. plug tobacco to manufacture cigarettes with. I forgot to get cigarettes yesterday.

(July 3, 1934)

Tom Brazil had been "squatting" on Hardy Island for 15 years before the American financier, Mr. L. A. McComber, first came to Desolation Sound on his big yacht, and he was there long after McComber's death, when the little paradise was despoiled by logging. While clearing a few acres to plant an orchard and a garden, Tom developed an astounding rapport with the wild world which delighted visitors and gave him the title "Friend of the Animals".

There is a story that Tom Brazil had a tame bear which he liked to ride as others would ride a horse. One day when he could not find his bear, he was forced to walk, but on his way home he came upon the bear asleep. He roused the animal, and when the bear seemed uncooperative, he scolded it into submission, climbed on its back and rode it home. Reaching his house, he was much surprised to discover his own tame bear asleep by the door.

Tom raised pheasants but didn't keep them penned, calling them at feeding times with a shrill whistle. Captain Brealeau of the tug *Beta II* relates that once when he was taking Tom to Powell River for supplies, a number of pheasants flew south, high above the tug. The captain leaned out of the window and said, jokingly, "Gee, if I only had a shotgun . . . "

"You don't need a gun," replied Tom. When he gave a shrill whistle, three of the birds wheeled out of the flock and landed at his feet.[2]

When McComber bought Hardy Island, he bought Tom with it. Tom served as caretaker and the McCombers built a summer home nearby. The island became a wild-life sanctuary, visitors being allowed to walk the cool forest trails, with the deer following them about. One deer named Billy would mince along the narrow planking of the float to strike each boat with a forehoof, looking for a handout. Then McComber died and Hardy Island was sold to a man who saw money in the fine stand of huge trees. Retained as caretaker, Tom Brazil had to watch the devastation of the logging and the death of the deer. In 1954 the island came into the possession of the Elk River Timber Company Ltd., whose owners stated that it was their intention not to log the island further. Tom Brazil was then 85.

> In the afternoon I went ashore and had a chat with Mr. Mc-Comber who I met on the trail. I had a yarn with Tom Brazil and while we were talking in his house a year-old buck came into the room and we fed it on bits of potato.
>
> (July 4, 1935)
>
> We are now anchored in the nice little bay opposite Mc-Comber's float. Amy produced a very fine supper: lamb chops, potatoes and turnip, stewed plums, cafe demi tasse. I went up the trail after supper and had a chat with Tom Brazil and Mrs. McComber. A two-year-old buck, a doe and fawn licked my

hands the while. My hands have not recovered from my tin-smithing and I believe deer licks are as good as Snap for remov-ing dirt.

(August 31, 1935)

We ran to the N.E. end of Blind Bay and anchored off Jud John-son's house. After some coffee and food, I went ashore and made myself known. Johnson, who used to live in Princess Louisa Inlet and who I have often heard of, came on board and we found him a perfect mine of information. He told us of quite a number of new pictographs, and explained some of the pictographic figures. He also told us where to find some good Indian stuff and said he would try and get some things for us. He is married to a Sechelt Indian woman and said he knew more of Indian legends and lore than white man's lore. We marked new pictograph sites on charts and two hours passed as five minutes.

(September 10, 1934)

Johnson is building a nice new house on some property he has bought. McComber arrived on the *Principia* and was busy for a time with Johnson at the new house. We went ashore to look at the house, and stepping out of the boat on to a flat rock, it top-pled over and shot me and the camera into the sea. I dried the camera at once and it did not seem much harmed. I took a photo of the Johnson family and we then left to go across the Inlet to take a photo of the pictos we visited some time ago. Afterward we went to Tom Brazil's place at Saltry Bay and tied at the float. Sandvold showed us over the place, a very nice spot. Sandvold is a great lover of flowers, and is an extremely interesting type of man. He was born in Glasgow, but moved when quite young, with his parents, to Norway before coming to this continent. He is a constructional engineer. His hobby is phrenology and all the other ologys connected with the sizing up of the characteristics of people he meets or sees going about their business. He says he very seldom gets fooled.

(September 1, 1935)

Saltry Bay, Tom Brazil's place. Sandvold showed us the garden and the lilacs which we sent them after we got home last year. They are doing very well. Tom was on the float and we had a yarn. He nearly caught us with one of his fancy stories, this time about Mac, but he was so serious that I was not taken in. We left at 12.45 after our friends had given us some peas, carrots, lettuce and onions from their garden. Amy cooked up the vegetables and we had our lunch about 2 o'clock as we were coming up the coast, truly a gastronomic delight.

(July 19, 1936)

Near the entrance to Blind Bay Amy noticed a pictograph about 13 feet above high water on a rock bluff. This, I feel sure, has not been recorded, so we stopped and took photos and made a sketch.

(July 3, 1934)

We ran on to Maud Bay, close to Thunder Bay and made fast to a boom where Roy Allan keeps his police boat. We went ashore and walked along a trail to a farm at Macray's Cove which we had seen from the sea as we passed round Scotch Fir Point. It was a pretty place.

(September 5, 1941)

The PGD 2 arrived alongside the float in the early hours of the morning, and we were surprised when we poked our heads out of *Toketie* after breakfast to see Roy Allen feeding two small raccoons on the float, and Tom Brazil there too, in his rowboat.

(September 6, 1941)

Into Sechelt Inlet:

Through Skookumchuck Narrows. At a point on Sechelt Peninsula opposite Boulder Id. we found a pictograph and another a little way further on.

(July 14, 1936)

Absorbed in the search for prehistoric Indian rock art, Barrow does not comment on the dangerous Skookumchuck, and it may be assumed that he passed through the narrows near slack water. Full, strong tides cause great whirlpools to form. Fifty-foot logs can be sucked down the middle and shot out again a quarter of a mile away. New boiling swirls constantly form. The roar and boom of this tumultuous water is deafening, with swarms of screaming seagulls adding to the pandemonium.

Just south of the Skookumchuck, on the west shore of Sechelt Inlet near Boulder Island, are two pictograph sites, the first of many sites recorded by the Barrows in Sechelt, Narrows and Salmon Inlets. Along the Inside Coast, the rock art and the middens are the most conspicuous legacies of the once-flourishing Indian cultures. The Sechelt people numbered 5,000 in 1792, according to an estimate made by Captain Vancouver, but by 1860 smallpox and tuberculosis had reduced that number to a pitiful 600.

> Arrived at Storm Bay and anchored. We met Mr. Stewart fishing and had a yarn and later on we pulled up anchor and tied up to his float in a snug bay near the head. Went up to see Mr. Stewart and he showed us his house which he had built, morticed doors, chairs, book-case, chest of drawers (the drawers were beautifully dovetailed) all of which he had made himself. Later on we put some lumber, windows and things on board which we were taking up to some friends of his near the head of Narrows Arm, Messrs. Morrison and Brown. We found Brown at home, and after anchoring we went ashore and saw the log cabin they are building. Morrison was up the river looking for a rod which an American had lost there yesterday. He said the American would give $100 if it were found. Brown took Amy off to try to catch one of the large trout that this place is famous for. When Amy came back without a trout, Morrison took her off to fish. They came back with a snapper. Later we took Morrison up to the mouth of the Tzoonye River [head of Narrows Inlet] near where he has a cabin. We anchored in very quiet water and talked till midnight, when Morrison went off to his cabin. He has had much trouble lately, his wife having died suddenly last month. He is interested in mining, and has a claim which he is working up the mountain near here.
>
> (July 15, 1936)

> Went over to the entrance to Narrows Arm and sketched and photographed the pictograph there. It was one that Stewart had marked on his sketch with six new places. We returned about 1 P.M. and Stewart came to lunch with us. Afterwards we all left for the head of the Inlet, picto hunting. We found two groups on the west side of the inlet about opposite Salmon Arm. These we passed by and went on to near Porpoise Bay where we found another group. As there was a bit of wind which did not admit of letting *Toketie* lie alongside the bluff, we went into a

bay and anchored and had tea. Stewart rowed me round to the picto and I took a photo and made a sketch. We then started on our return to Storm Bay, finding two more groups on the east side of the Inlet.

(August 27, 1936)

We went to the Jap store at Skookumchuck Narrows and got bread, meat and a few other things. Stewart left to see the local blacksmith about a new rudder for his gasboat. Jud Johnson arrived in a big launch full of Indians on their way to Vancouver.

(August 30, 1936)

Leaving Sechelt Inlet and looking for a quiet anchorage, the Barrows crossed Jervis Inlet and ran into Hotham Sound.

We are anchored in a spot we have never rested in before. It is nice and quiet and we seem to be the only inhabitants of the Sound. We had intended going to a bay where we were some years ago, where we got some fruit in a deserted orchard, but I made a mistake. We should have gone to the head of St. Vincent Bay. The news which we get over the radio from Europe is very disturbing, but we can't do much about it here in Hotham Sound.

(September 8, 1938)

We passed a very quiet night. There was a little rain. In the morning we explored by the creek which emptied into the bay on the right. It was too wet in the bush to go any distance. We then went down the Sound a mile or two and went ashore at an old logging camp. At 12.15 we went on to the head of St. Vincent Bay and anchored where we were in 1936. There were two boats in the little bay, and three men were over at the old orchard across the bay, picking apples and prunes. When they came back to the boats we had a talk, and found that one of them, Mr. Day, had bought the property close to where we are anchored, since we were here last. He fishes up north in the summer, and stays here in the winter. He has a fine garden and has started fixing up the house. In the afternoon we went across the bay to the old house with the orchard and picked a few prunes. There are four big prune trees laden with fruit and a lot of it will go to waste. Day came over too and picked some to make prune wine. There are a lot of apples too. The orchard and garden are on an old Indian house site, and Day said the owner dug up a lot of Indian stuff and sold it to a timber cruiser for $10. The owner, who is 95, does not live here any more. Day came to supper with us. He wants to put in a water-wheel in his stream, for charging his radio batteries. It is an ideal spot for such a wheel, plenty of drop and enough water. Day used to live close to the Stewarts in Storm Bay, Sechelt Inlet.

(September 9, 1938)

We went ashore after morning tea and had a yarn with George Day, looked over his garden and house, and said good-bye. On going back to *Toketie*, Mr. Walter Day, no relation to George Day, rowed into the bay from the old man's house nearby, where he is living. He talked a while, said we could have all the prunes we wanted, and the hammer we looked at yesterday. This was too good to pass up, so after lunch we rowed over and got the hammer and prunes. Also some small greengage plums. Walter Day said the 95-year-old man found a lot of Indian stuff when he dug over his orchard, including several quite long greenstone adzes or chisels. Also the jaw bone, complete with teeth, of an enormous man. Day is going to let me know if he finds anything. Also, a boy who was there, who lives in the bay, is going to hunt. I had two games of crib with Day and one with the boy and got beaten every time. I left my pack of cards for them as the pips on theirs were pretty hard to see, and the joker had to do duty for the eight of diamonds. Mr. Walter Day had had trouble the day before with bears raiding his orchard.

(September 10, 1938)

Jervis Inlet is roughly a mile wide, with mountains rising straight up, 5,000 to 8,000 feet on either side. There are very few places for safe anchoring and little shelter from the winds that blow up the inlet in the summer mornings and down the inlet in late afternoon. In winter Jervis Inlet is especially dangerous because there are such strong "williwaws" that small boats cannot make headway against them. Lingering too long in St. Vincent Bay, the *Toketie* had a rough run to Vancouver Bay.

We ran through fog and torrential rain to Vancouver Bay where we arrived at 5 P.M. The rain comes down in buckets full and dances up off the sea. I have never seen it rain so hard.

Plates and pans are in use in the cabin under the windows to catch drips, but very few boats would be tight in weather like this. Rupert Hagman, one of the caretakers from the logging camp, came down and had a yarn when we arrived. We fed him on beer and cake. He says there is good anchorage inside the mouth of Britton River in about 12 feet, low tide, but one has to wait for high water to go over the bar at the mouth. Very good supper: boiled ling cod, white sauce (made of barley meal, onion, salt, butter), canned peas, cherries, coffee. Amy had Ryvita with above, but I don't like cardboard. Our bread has gone mouldy on us.

(July 1, 1933)

Joe asked us to breakfast and we had some magnificent hot cakes and coffee. Also fresh strawberries from Joe's garden. I washed my clothes up at the camp – lots of hot water and a line behind one of the buildings for drying. We met Mr. Fisher who has lived in Vancouver Bay for a long time. He was in the Chinese Customs for many years and is logging here.

(June 26, 1935)

Most of the yachts heading north up Jervis Inlet are going to one of the most delightful of tiny inlets – Princess Louisa. Half-way up the farthest reach of Jervis Inlet (the Queen's Reach), a narrow, hidden opening only 60 feet wide admits a rush of tide into the five-mile-long fiord of Princess Louisa Inlet. On the north side of this dramatic entrance there is a beautiful log building which was built as a wilderness hotel for Hollywood stars. When the Barrows came to Princess Louisa Inlet, this spot was occupied by Casper and his cats.

When the inlet is calm its surface is a mirror that reflects the mile-high vertical granite walls, so that the sky below seems as far under as the sky is high above. When the surface is opaque, the sailor feels like a tiny ant at the bottom of a high-sided box, his or her head constantly bending back – far back – to look up and up. Until mid-June, the melting snows create more than 60 waterfalls. The largest, Chatterbox Falls at the head of the inlet, comes swiftly down the mountains and then slides and plunges the last 120 feet over greasy green moss where many have ventured too close and been killed.

On the 1933 visit to the inlet, the Barrows stopped in the Queen's Reach to record pictographs:

> Stopped three miles south of Patrick Point and I sketched the pictographs we could not find when we came up before. Too late in the day to take a photo. We also found the single figure further down the Inlet. We arrived at the entrance to Princess Louisa Inlet as it got dark, but managed to make our way to the island where we usually tie up, and did not hit any driftwood. The searchlight was most useful in picking up the small bay where we lie. There are so many shadows at night in this Inlet; it is like navigating at the bottom of a deep well.
>
> (September 8, 1933)

> After breakfast Amy did the family wash on board, and there is every prospect of the clothes drying well, the day being bright and sunny. I believe we are too late for blueberries but I have not been ashore to investigate. The underbrush is still very wet with dew. We went ashore and hung up the clothes and after lunch johnsoned up to the waterfall to see Macdonald. He, however, was away, but a girl was in the house. This was her first visit to the inlet and she was thrilled with everything, especially Macdonald's log house which is very nice: a big living room, very lofty and the logs oiled. There is a huge fireplace. The smaller rooms open off the large room. The house is delightful, both inside and out. We then johnsoned down to Casper's, but found him away, a note on the door saying "Back at 5 o'clock". However, remembering that old guy on Galiano Island who put "Back at 5 o'clock" on his door and went to California on a trip for three months, we only waited until 5, and as Casper did not return, we left to take in the washing and get supper. I picked a nice feed of blueberries and huckleberries. These were delicious stewed.
>
> (September 9, 1933)

> Had a yarn with Casper, who had been over at the Whitakers at Patrick Pt. yesterday. We ran up to Macdonald's. Casper now has 14 cats, one less than on our last visit.
>
> (September 10, 1933)

> The *Croesus* was there and Mrs. Blanchet with her party, so we

did not land, as Macdonald has so many visitors. Casper has
been smoking tea for the past two weeks so I was glad we had
brought him up some tobacco. Amy found a couple of arrow-
heads in Casper's garden.

(June 25, 1933)

J. F. Macdonald, known on the coast as "Mac", or "The Man from
California", first came to this remote place in 1905, a boy on his
uncle's yacht. He could never afterwards get Princess Louisa Inlet
out of his mind. Twenty-five years later, when he had struck it rich
prospecting in Nevada, he pre-empted the 45 acres at the head of
the inlet and built a log house. As a first intruder into this unique
place, he was to prove himself a worthy tenant. For many years he
welcomed visitors, entertaining them in his house. After the house
burned in 1940, he lived on a houseboat, enjoying many good chess
matches with anyone who wished to play. Determined that "this
beautiful peaceful haven should never belong to one individual", in
1953 he placed the land in trust with the Princess Louisa Interna-
tional Society, a yachtsmen's association.[3] They in turn gave the
land in 1963 to the people of British Columbia, to be a marine park
supervised by the Parks Branch of the provincial government.

In her book *The Curve of Time* Muriel Wylie Blanchet, who was
one of the too-many visitors at Mac's when the Barrows arrived
with Casper, has described Mac's house, built of peeled cedar logs
with a big main room, 40 by 20 feet, dominated by a great granite
fireplace. Mrs. Blanchet's book also describes voyages during the
Thirties, to many of the same places visited by the Barrows. In the
winter she lived at Curteis Point, not far from the Barrows' home in
North Saanich. Left a widow at the age of 36, she took her five children northwards on summer cruises in a 25-foot boat, the *Caprice*.
At Princess Louisa, the Blanchets camped at Trapper's Rock to the
south of Chatterbox Falls, where a little stream of ice-cold spring
water comes out on the shore.

> We went to see Casper, to get him to go and get some teeth out
> as he has suffered a lot lately from them. He gave us some dried
> bearmeat and the ladder he had made for me yesterday, for
> climbing up to pictographs. We then went to the big group of
> pictos opposite Ruby Creek and at the right moment a hand
> logger came along to this spot to cruise for timber, and he
> helped me up to the ledge and took my camera up. I took some
> close-up photos and found some small stones all with pigment

on them, which I took. I left quite a lot behind. Then we visited
two small groups to the south of the big group, and after that
crossed the inlet to the two groups just south of Ruby Creek,
which I took photos of and sketched. We met Mr. Macnaugh-
ton, who lives in Ruby Creek Bay and hand logs, and we are
now, at 7.15, tied up to his boom and just going to have supper.

(June 25, 1933)

Francis Barrow mailed three of the painted stones to Harlan
Smith at the National Museum, gave two to William Newcombe,
and kept several in his own collection which was later given to the
Provincial Museum. It has been reported that young women of the
Interior Salish groups, as part of their puberty ceremonies, painted
figures on small stones. At Kuper Island in the Gulf Islands, the Salish people used painted stones in connection with initiation rites
of new dancers, the stones being dropped into water used to
cleanse and purify the initiates. Pamela Amoss' study of Coast Salish spirit dancing includes a description of the use of certain
stones to detect the presence of evil spirits in the dance house. The
painted stones found by Barrow are similar implements of power.

Mac came with us up the inlet picto hunting. We found a new
group and then we moved to the big group. We then went on
to the Indian village and had a yarn with the inhabitants. Later
we walked along the trail to the junction of the two rivers, a
very pretty spot and a splendid place for trout fishing. Humpies
were making their way up the river.

(September 3, 1935)

Paid Casper a visit and he cut my hair in a very professional
manner. Afterwards we went up to Mac's house and Amy
rested on the best settle in front of the fire and Mac and I
played chess. I am quite out of practice and lost both games.

(September 4, 1939)

Went up to see Macdonald. Mrs. Blanchet's children saw a bear
this morning, not far from the waterfall. After returning to our
tie up for lunch, we rowed across to one of the creeks and
made a fire on the beach and washed a fine batch of clothes.
We heated up water in two buckets, and after washing the
clothes the creek did the rinsing act.

(June 27, 1933)

We were entertained by watching a man jacking Mac's hut onto a float so that the Eliels can use it at the property they have bought in the Inlet, while their house is being built. The man was an expert at his job and only took two days to lash the float together and put the house on it. We made fast to Macdonald's boom and had supper at 5.30 P.M.: tongue, baby beets, asparagus tips, toast (the bread has mildewed with the damp) followed by pectenized turnip which claims to be cherry jam. Mac and his nephew came down to the float about 6 P.M. to dine on board the big motor cruiser *Polaris* of San Francisco. She was here when we were here last year, and Mac asked us if we had any idea of the name of the owner, as he had forgotten it. We could not help him out, but I hope he will eventually discover his host's name.

(July 9, 1936)

We rowed round the rock and fished without luck, and then went ashore and talked to a man who was taking photographs. He had a Bucher camera by the same maker as mine, but a ¼ plate. He turned out to be Mr. Easthope from Vancouver. We talked cameras, and Mr. Easthope said he was a professional photographer in Victoria before he moved to Vancouver to build engines.

(July 12, 1938)

Francis Barrow failed to note whether it was Percy "Peck" Easthope or his brother George whom he encountered at Princess Louisa Inlet. Their father, Ernest Easthope, head of this inventive family, developed the first ball bearing for a bicycle. In 1880, in Wolverhampton, Staffordshire, 20 years before the Wright brothers, this same Mr. Easthope tried to build a flying machine with two pedal-powered fans (one vertical, one horizontal—a bicycle-helicopter). Emigrating to British Columbia, the Easthopes settled at a spot which is now the corner of Kingsway and Edmonds Street in Burnaby.

Son Vincent Easthope, working with his father in a bicycle shop they had established on Hastings Street, saw an account of an American motor called the Roberts motor, which was built about 1900. Vince and his father then made a small motor (about a half-horsepower) which was used to propel a Peterborough canoe, the first gasboat in Vancouver. It ran on petrol, which became available about 1900. Next they built a three-horsepower cast-iron motor, which was installed in the *Swan,* an 18-foot boat built by Dan Martin. By this time there was a great deal of interest in their experiments and many fishermen wanted motors. Up until this time the fishing boats had only sails and oars. In a *Raincoast Chronicles* article, Peck Easthope described the gillnet fleet in the days before the Easthope motor. The Columbia River fishing boats set out, about 2,000 strong, "all with their sails up fannin' out over the river just like a great big flock of gulls. The sun glowing the sails – it was a beautiful sight. A beautiful sight. All them boats to put motors in, you see."[4]

When Vince Easthope died during an operation, it was a terrible blow to the family, but young Ernest came in to take his place. There were new partners from outside the family, and the business faltered. Then George Easthope, an engineer, and his brother Peck, a dairy farmer, decided to begin again, this time using Model T Ford motor parts to make the Easthope motor which became so popular on the west coast. They ran the business from 1914 until their retirement in 1953, watching their motor revolutionize the fishing industry. In top years they sold about a hundred motors, all built in their shop at 1747 West Georgia in Vancouver, where they employed about 50 men. Some of their motors are still going.

> We went up to the waterfall about eleven and met Mac and his wife and step-daughter. The day improved and I took some movies. Very colourful were those of Mac's daughter and some girls off the boats in bright woven garments that the Macs had got when they were in Guatemala last winter. To add to our trouble of a dead battery, I found a leak in the gas line to the engine, which I shall have to do something about.
>
> (August 2, 1940)

> When I tried to tighten up the nipple on the gas line, it broke in half. I was lucky to be able to get a new nipple from the owner of the *Riptide* of Seattle, and I spent the morning getting the two broken halves out of the union and elbow. I soldered the joints and had the pipe in place again before lunch. In the afternoon I took some movies of the waterfall. Mac and Pat happened to come along in their canoe and made a nice foreground for the shot. We explored the cave just above us, a splendid camp site, a huge overhanging boulder. Amy took me

for a row before supper. Pat came over in the evening to invite us to a campfire party at the Mac's cabin and we rowed over soon after and found a lot of people from the various boats gathered round the open fireplace outside the cabin. They were a friendly and jolly crowd. Amy sat next Mrs. MacMichen and Jackson her son came and we at last met our Shoal Harbour neighbours. There were songs, violin numbers, a recitation, a dance by two of the youngsters and a play, Pat being the author. Mac gave us an interesting account of the early Indians of Princess Louisa Inlet and their legends, and I was called on to say something about the rock paintings on the coast, but I am afraid my contribution to the evening's entertainment was decidedly weak.

(August 3, 1940)

Took some movies of Mac and Mrs. M. in the Foldbot which they got last year in Germany. Tried to start the engine but found the jinx has not left us yet. There was an air-lock in the gas line and I spent hours trying to get the gas to flow. Blowing into the tank, I got a mouthful and an eyeful which was not at all pleasant. After hours of struggling, I managed to get the engine to run, and we started down the inlet. Anchored just inside the entrance. It is very peaceful here, but the anchor-chain groans on the rocks and we get twisted round and round with the surge. I am wondering if the jinx is going to fix our anchor among the rocks so that we cannot haul it up again.

(August 4, 1940)

The next morning the anchor came up and *Toketie* ran south down Jervis Inlet with the repaired gas line feeding the throbbing motor. Rounding Scotch Fir Point at the entrance to Jervis Inlet, the little ship turned north up Malaspina Strait, stopping at Texada Island, the whale-shaped island that forms the long, high, western wall of the strait. The backbone of Texada Island rises to 2,900 feet, presenting a steep, forbidding face on both east and west sides. No Indians have lived there, for they say that the island rose out of the sea and will one day sink back under the waves.

Discovered and named by the Spaniards in 1791, the island was first inhabited by whalers, who used Blubber Bay as a whaling station in the days when whales were plentiful in this area. The whalers were gone when, about 1870, Harry Trim came to shelter in the only hospitable part of the Texada coast, at the north end, where Sturt Bay and Blubber Bay offer a safe anchorage. Trim walked ashore, scuffed up the earth and was surprised to discover iron ore. Trim's machinations led to the notorious "Texada Scandal" which involved Premier Amor de Cosmos and some of his friends. A Royal Commission exonerated them for lack of evidence, but when the dust of controversy settled, no one seemed eager to risk a development project except some Americans. In 1897 the Vananda Copper and Gold Company was formed, named after a New York journalist. The townsite was laid out, five miles from the north end of the island, and three mines were started. By 1900 there were 3,000 people on Texada. The boom reached its peak during the First World War, when many mines were in operation—the Copper Queen, the Marble Bay, the Cornell, the Malaspina, the Golden Slipper, the Little Billy and others. At Vananda wooden sidewalks ran everywhere to connect the houses and bunkhouses with three saloons, a church, a school, a newspaper office (the *Coast Miner*) and, impressively, an opera house. Vananda had liquor, music and the confidence that it would last forever. By 1916 Marble Bay mine's 1500-foot shaft had tunnelled far under Malaspina Strait.

The war ended, the market for iron collapsed, the mines closed and Vananda became the ghost town that the Barrows visited in 1935. But a first lime kiln had been built at Blubber Bay in 1887, and the lime quarrying went quietly on. In 1927 the British Columbia Cement Company amalgamated with the Pacific Lime Company at Blubber Bay, shipping raw lime to the cement plant at Bamberton. When the Barrows were eating supper aboard the *Toketie* at Blubber Bay they were disturbed by the noise of winches loading lime aboard the *S.S. Kingsley.*

Not everyone abandoned Texada when the boom collapsed. Some turned to farming, for the lime in the soil produced excellent gardens. The climate helped, for some quirk of air currents gives Texada more sunshine and less rain than the nearby mainland. Interior lakes provided limited irrigation. Sheep foraged on the steep slopes and there was good fishing just offshore.

> Ran to Vananda where we had lunch: cabbage, potatoes and ham, followed by stewed plums and cornflower blacman(ge or che, I don't know). We rather wanted to go over the road to

Gillies Bay and two miles further on to see Bill Horth, but
neither of the storekeepers were able today to take their cars
out, so we have yet to see the world's worst road. Vananda, that
ghost town, looked so dead that we went on to Blubber Bay and
made fast to a boom of logs in front of the lime works. As we
were having supper (some of Amy's nice cod, boiled, with
sauce) *S.S. Kingsley* came alongside the wharf and they started
to load lime. I expect the winches will be going all night. There
was a fresh N.W. breeze as we came up Malaspina Strait.

(July 6, 1935)

We went up to the store and renewed supplies and got off some
mail, the *Chelohsin* calling this evening. We went round into
Marble Bay and are now made fast to a float opposite the lime-
stone quarry. We went for a walk after supper and bought
some vegetables from a man who had a wonderful garden, as
indeed all the vegetable gardens are here. Great big cabbages
and high standing corn and everything about as good as could
be. Our friend said it was the lime in the soil which made it so
fertile.

(July 23, 1938)

Anchored close to the B.C. Cement Works. I wanted to see Bill
Addison who lives close by and who the store-keeper at Vananda said was a good electrician. The object of our visit was to
get him to step up the output of the Westinghouse generator.
Addison found some of the connections in the instrument
board loose and corroded and the base socket of the fuse was
just about finished. We rowed across to the lime works and I
was fortunate to get a new base and eight fuses, the fuses cost-
ing 15 cents for four. This was indeed luck as I had forgotten to
bring spare fuses when we left home and I would not have had
the opportunity of getting them further up the coast. Addison
altered three of the ground wires which was a great improve-
ment and the horn works readily now, which it has not done
for years. Not that I use that instrument often. He cleaned the
commutator on the Auto generator and it produced 4 amps
when the motor ran. However, when we left with both gener-
ators running, the meter only showed 8 amps. I will have to see
to that, as it is not enough.

(July 24, 1938)

I took some movies of the men working in the lime quarry. I sent our door key to Will and asked him to be good enough to send the spare gasket for the engine to Refuge Cove as there is water on the valves and the sparkplugs when the engine gets cold after a run. The present gasket is evidently defective. We talked to a fisherman, Mr. Lee, an Australian, close by. As it got dusk, Brown Horth came in, with his family.

(August 11, 1940)

We made fast at our usual anchorage (Marble Bay) and after supper walked up to Mr. Ammundson's and got some vegetables from his splendid garden. He returned with us and had several games of crib with me.

(August 12, 1940)

From Texada it is a run of only a few minutes to Powell River on the mainland.

Went ashore at Powell River to do some shopping and smelt a new evil smell every hundred yards or so, from the large paper works. We met by chance the Conners at whose logging float we tied up last year, at the N. end of Waddington Channel. They are now at Prussian Id. and invited us to look them up when we are near there. It was hot and dusty and we were glad to get back to the boat at 1 o'clock, when a mechanic came down from the garage to look at the carburetor, which has not been working very well lately. He took it apart and found the idling jet was clogged up. We put it in good shape, and we then looked at the Johnson overboard motor which has only been working on one cylinder lately. We found the coil was finished and he is getting a new one from Vancouver.

(July 9, 1934)

"The forests of Powell River area have been read all over the world," wrote Stephen E. Hilson in *Exploring Puget Sound and British Columbia.* "The local papermill has been the world's largest single unit papermill, producing millions of tons of newsprint for the world market."[5] The idea of a papermill originated with William Hewartson, a retired English paper maker in Victoria. He interested Herbert Carmichael in the project and they established a mill at Port Alberni, which produced the first reel of paper in British Columbia in 1894. However, as the equipment was antiquated and designed to make pulp from rags, not wood, the mill was closed in 1896 and Carmichael, in company with Bertie Boyd, was sent to find a better mill site. Hiring Albert Tranfield and his sailboat, the young men examined every creek and river flowing into Howe Sound, Hotham Sound, Jervis Inlet and north to Bute Inlet. They were well pleased to find Powell River Falls with 50,000 untamed horse power, so easy of access and so close to tide water, and the great reservoir of Powell Lake in the mountains behind. In the power struggle over the new mill, American money and Minneapolis businessmen soon replaced the Canadians. The new mill began producing newsprint in 1912. In the years when the Barrows sniffed the smell of success at Powell River, the great mill was flanked by a new company town where the Depression rested lightly; there was a payroll of $2,500,000 in 1931.

Leaving Powell River, the Barrows entered the Desolation Sound area, so popular with modern yachtsmen, where the tides from north and south meet, their force diminished, their sun-warmed waters delightful for swimming.

Us. (Francis and Amy Barrow, North Saanich, date unknown.)

The Hughes and ourselves, Jedidiah Island, 1938.

The Whites and ourselves, Squitty Bay, Lasqueti Island, 1936.

Dr. and Mrs. Johnston, St. Mary's Hospital, Pender Harbour, 1940.

The Mitchells, Pender Harbour, 1940.

Joe Gonsalves and his daughter, Mrs. Dames, 1938.

The Johnson family of Blind Bay, 1935.

Mr. Stewart, Storm Bay, Sechelt Inlet, 1936.

George Day, St. Vincent Bay, 1938.

Brown's camp, Narrows Arm, 1936.

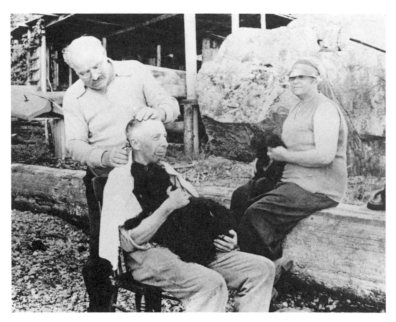

Casper cuts my hair, Princess Louisa Inlet, 1935.

Amy doing the laundry.

The Macdonalds in their foldboat, Princess Louisa Inlet, 1940.

Amy and the Parrish family, 1936.

Ed Berglund and us, Thors Cove, Malaspina Inlet, 1936.

Toketie, Malaspina Inlet, 1935.

Saulter and Frank. This looks like the manufacture of hooch, but is nothing worse than a steam box for bending planks for their boat. 1934.

Phil Lavigne, Prideaux Haven, 1938.

Wood and Armitage and Toby at Refuge Cove, 1934.

At the Wood, Armitage and Sheldon camp, Pendrell Sound, 1938.

CHAPTER FOUR

Happily the Barrows abandoned the rank air of Powell River to sniff the calm coolness of a placid morning, as the prow of the *Toketie* cut into the glassy sea. An hour's run northward brought them to Lund:

> Finn Bay at Lund, where we made fast to a float where there was plenty of room. This is a nice sheltered bay, but we have never bccn in it before. We rowed to the government float, thinking that we could get dinner at the hotel. We were sent over to a light lunch counter connected with Thulim's Store on the wharf, where we got nothing more exciting than tomato sandwiches and tca and ice cream.
>
> (September 4, 1941)

Perhaps the best known of the many Swedish families of the coast was the Thulin family of Lund, the name they chose for their settlement, after their home city in Sweden. Charles Thulin arrived first, in 1884, but his brother Frederick was only two years behind him. By 1895 they had opened the Malaspina Hotel, holding the first hotel licence on the coast north of Vancouver. This hotel was destroyed by fire in 1919, long before the Barrow visit. Not satisfied with one settlement and one hotel, the Thulin brothers put lumber and a horse on a scow and crossed the strait to Campbell River, where they were again the first white people to settle. Here and at Lund they logged with oxen, founding communities that flourished. Later they built the old Willows Hotel at Campbell River. At Lund in 1901, Fred Thulin built a structure near the dock which he called the Pavilion; the following year it was converted to the store and café which gave the Barrows the nondescript tomato sandwiches. By this time the Thulins were not only farmers, loggers, hotel owners, shopkeepers and restaurateurs; they also owned a gas station, a fish-buying station and an insurance office, and were notaries public.

Opposite Lund lies crescent-shaped Savary Island, fringed with sand beaches, destined from the moment of its discovery to be a holiday place. Archibald Menzies, the naturalist on Captain Vancouver's expedition in 1792 reports that Lieutenant Puget and Mr. Whidbey "stopped for the evening on one of the islands and pitched tents in a delightful plain, with a fine smooth beach before it for the boats, that rendered the situation both desirable and pleasant and such as the men had seldom enjoyed."[1] The island was Savary.

> Savary Id. Made fast alongside Spilsbury's boat. I wanted to talk with him about radios and see if he had one suitable for our boat, which would not use so much juice as our old Philco, which apart from this is as good as ever. The *Lady Cynthia* was at the wharf, having unloaded a mass of holiday makers from Vancouver. She left with the gang at 3.30, our time, and very soon after we left for Bliss Landing.
>
> (July 31, 1941)

To add the perfect touch to this holiday island, Savary has undiscovered buried treasure. In the 1870s there was a trading post on the island run by a man named Jack Green, who was observed to have in his possession a large amount of money. He was murdered for this wealth by two men who were later caught and hanged, but the money was never found, and the murderers insisted that they had not found it either.

Savary Island has another claim to fame: Jim Spilsbury, whose home was on Savary, and his partner, Jim Hepburn, were the radio experts of the coast, and then, almost inadvertently, they founded Queen Charlotte Airlines. In the ninth *Raincoast Chronicles,* Spilsbury relates that when radio telephones became available, every logging camp, cannery, store and homestead wanted to have one of these remarkable new devices. Spilsbury and Hepburn serviced the coast by boat until wartime gasoline rationing made this difficult. Jim's cousin Rupert, an ex-barnstorming, ex-trans-Atlantic ferry command pilot, suggested getting a plane.

When the company decided to establish service to the Queen Charlotte Islands they needed a Stranraer flying boat, which cost $50,000. Seeking backing for a loan from the Powell River Company, they were required to do a test run to the Charlottes with 20 passengers before the deal was signed. Spilsbury relates that when they headed north in a southeast gale they discovered that none of the instruments worked. Landing the Stranraer at Savary Island, the flight engineer, Hank Elwin, managed to climb to the upper wing, 12 feet above, to reach the pedo head, the tube which supplies air pressure to the instruments. There he found that a condom had been taped over the opening to keep dirt out when the aircraft was in storage. When he removed it, the instruments sprang to life.

Queen Charlotte Airlines grew with surprising rapidity. Spilsbury had a tiger by the tail, for the post-war years on the Inside Coast were a brief boom period. In Spilsbury's words, "Just looking at a place like Minstrel Island, which today boasts about three families total—in the late forties we were hauling 20 and 40 people a day in and out of that place."[2] When he finally sold out in 1955, he returned to the radio business for another 25 years.

Leaving Spilsbury at Savary Island, Barrow headed the *Toketie* north, toward Bliss Landing.

> Just before we turned into Bliss Landing, Parrish and his family passed in a speed boat which they were taking up to the Yacultas from Vancouver. They stopped at Bliss Landing and we

had a yarn. Some pleasant people, a fellow and his wife, arrived while we were there, from Vancouver, in a very roomy open small sail boat, on their way to the Alert Bay area. They had a canvas cabin complete with windows for putting up at night. Mr. Young, the store-keeper, received us graciously and we made some purchases and got gas. The name of the Vancouver sail boat was *Underwing*. I took a photo of the Indian carved wooden bear head which I had looked at before, but I think Young wants too much for it.

(July 7, 1935)

We then went to Turner Bay, very near by, and found Ed Berglund at home. After a chat Ed and I started a game of crib when Anderson, who owns the property, came in. We went over to the Andersons' house and had a three-handed game of crib till supper time, the Andersons insisting that Amy and I should stay to the meal. They have a nice place and a good garden and orchard, more fruit than I have seen anywhere.

(September 8, 1940)

Bliss Landing. We got some things at the store and met Clarence Cabeen who came in with his boat, on his way home to Minstrel Island. He had been down to Vancouver to buy a big second-hand truck engine, and had gone to Uclulet to see if he liked that part of the world sufficiently to start a machine shop there. He was, however, not much impressed. The tinsmith from Blind Creek also came in.

(August 1, 1941)

The *Lady Cecilia* came in during the early hours of the morning and later a Shell Oil boat. It rained heavily all night and the drip from my window ran into my sleeping bag and I found my feet in cold water. It is blowing S.E. outside, but this seems to be a sheltered spot. The packer *Quathiaski* came in on her way to Kanish Bay and I had a chat with Billy Law. He said he had heard of some carvings on the rocks at Open Bay, of ships, and he is going to let me know more about them. He said since the cannery at Quathiaski Cove burnt down last week they have to run with their fish to Steveston. Young Jack from Refuge Cove came in with his speed-boat and was surprised to see us. After a rather rainy day it cleared up in the evening, the moon shining brightly, and stars, and the glass going up to 29.80.

(September 3, 1941)

We got a stack of mail and had a yarn with Mr. Young and his family. I got some things at Young's store and gasoline and we pulled out for Grace Harbour at 7.10 and reached that quiet anchorage in an hour.

(July 9, 1941)

Grace Harbour is in Malaspina Inlet. In the morning the Barrows set off to explore Trevenon Bay, only a few minutes from Grace Harbour.

To the head of Trevenon Bay where we landed and found a garden. We walked along a trail and later came to buildings. Here we met a family named Crowther, from Hertfordshire. We bought some eggs and they showed us the garden by the house. We had a lot to talk about and they seemed pleased to see us. They have a nice log house, half built. A cougar killed one of their goats lately and attacked the Crowther's 14-year-old daughter, but their dog went for it and saved her from a bad mauling. The dog has a bad wound on its head. We got back to *Toketie* after dark. As I write this, we are enjoying a concert of chamber music from Portland KEX. Reception is very good. The Crowthers tell us there are some skulls lying round on one of the three islands at the mouth of Trevenon Bay. We will have to see about this tomorrow, as Bill Newcombe in his letter I got at Pender Harbour says skulls of the Salish and Kwakiutl are poorly represented at Ottawa and a small series would be acceptable. I can't fill up *Toketie* with skulls as we have not much room, but if we find any I can very easily mail them to W.A.N. as we are only six miles from Bliss Landing where there is a post office. 11 P.M. Time to hit the hay.

(July 4, 1933)

"We always enjoy Newcombe's company on the occasions when he can get away with us," Barrow wrote to Harlan Smith. "He is a splendid chap to play round in a boat with."[3] T. W. Paterson has described Billy Newcombe as "the lonely figure with bushy hair and prominent nose which daily haunted the Dallas Road beaches [in

Victoria], salvaging driftwood."⁴ In the house of this recluse was
what would later be labelled "the internationally famous Newcombe Collection", an outstanding assemblage of Indian artifacts.
There were also rare books, papers and photographs, as well as
almost a hundred Emily Carr paintings, for Newcombe was her
friend. He helped her with handyman tasks, crated her paintings
with the driftwood he had found on the beach and taught her the
legends and culture of the Indians whose totems she painted, just
as he taught Francis Barrow. The paintings, the artifacts and the
papers were all left by Billy Newcombe to the people of British Columbia, and now form part of the museum and archives collections. As a boy Newcombe accompanied his father, Dr. C. F. Newcombe, on visits upcoast to buy Indian art and artifacts. After his
father's death in 1924, Billy worked as an assistant biologist at the
museum until he was dismissed, which Barrow and others considered an injustice. Amy and Francis Barrow loved and appre-
ciated this shy, intelligent and sensitive man.

> Went over in the row boat, Johnson propelling, to Alton Id.
> When we stopped the Johnson and looked up at the island we
> were surprised to see two cougars watching us, about the size
> of large Airedales. They would have been an easy shot, had one
> a rifle. We did not land, but went over to the Isbester Ids. to
> look for skulls, but no luck. We found the remains of an old
> fish-trap between two of them. After lunch we johnsoned to
> the Crowthers and told them about the cougars on Alton Id.
> Mr. and Mrs. Crowther and Dick landed with their rifles but
> could not locate the cougars. The brush is very thick in places
> and I think they probably swam across from the island after we
> saw them. However, there were their tracks on the island and
> those of a large cougar. We then went to Isbester Id. and Dick
> showed us where he found the skull. There was a lively nest of
> hornets just by it, and we had no chance of getting the lower
> jaw even if it had been there. We were lucky to get the upper
> half without getting stung. We towed the Crowthers back to
> their place at the end of Trevenon Bay and returned to our an-
> chorage in Grace Harbour, where we had supper.
>
> (July 5, 1933)

The fish traps were walls of large and small stones, built at the
low tide line at the mouths of streams or small inlets, or on

beaches. The spawning salmon swam over the rock walls at high tide and were trapped when the tide went down.

The Crowthers' 14-year-old daughter, Nancy, was destined to have many more encounters with the wily cougars, for her father was already going blind when the Barrows visited him in 1933. It was Nancy who became a deadly shot, to protect the goats, dogs and poultry. Nancy was only a child when her parents arrived on the British Columbia coast. She had trudged behind them when they had to blaze a trail from Powell River to reach the 135 acres they had bought for ten dollars, in 1927. "There were 57 children in the inlet when we first came here," Nancy told a *Province* newspaper reporter in 1973. "Now there are two."[5]

Nancy spoke to the reporter in the log cabin which the Crowther family had built. Although she now had a generator, she did not use it, for she enjoyed the quiet. She preferred the soft light from her coal-oil lamps and a wood stove still heated the house, but she did turn on a battery radio every day to hear the world news. After her parents died, Nancy stayed on, with seven dogs and other animals. "Some-times I get lonely too, but the moment I sit down my dogs feel they should get some attention, so that's the end of being lonely."[6] This sturdy middle-aged lady with an English accent harvested her own oysters and clams, preserved fruit from the orchard, butchered her own chickens, made cheese from the milk of her goats and kept a few hives of bees for the honey. She had to buy grain, wheat and oats for the livestock. Across the bay was an oyster-processing plant where she could get work during the winter, to pay the taxes and buy the grains. Through the years she had to shoot bear and cougar, "otherwise the cougars get so tame they come right up to the house. Last year one stole three geese."[7] A neighbour, Axel Hansen, lost 30 goats to cougar in one night.

> After breakfast we went ashore at the old Kekaekae village and found a few Hudsons Bay trade beads on the beach. Later in the morning—no, it was early in the afternoon—we went to Thors Cove and visited Ed Berglund. He showed us his garden, his vegetables being as fine as ever. He has a splendid water supply, the water running all the time into a tub, an unfailing flow in the dryest years. He gave us some beans and lettuce. Also four very good arrow points which he had found this year in his garden. He gave us some good Indian stone implements last year

too. Amy did some washing on the float, water being so plentiful, and then she had a bathe, the water being quite warm. Ed
came to supper with us. We listened to the tug boats sending in
their radio messages and reporting to headquarters on the
weather. Radio reception is very good here, and stations come
in by the dozen. We get the *Province* news very clearly, and in
this out-of-the-way spot hear what is happening in England and
other parts of the world.

(July 10, 1934)

At 8.45 A.M. we took Ed over to Roos' Bay [Okeover Arm, at the
head of Malaspina Inlet] as he was going to Lund for his
monthly supply of grub, and no sooner had we landed than
Crowther came along and asked us to run six sacks of feed up
the arm to his home. We did this, and returned with him to
Roos' float.

(July 9, 1935)

When writer Will Dawson was cruising in Okeover Arm in the
1960s, he met Mrs. John Oscar Roos, who told him how she had
come as a young wife to help her husband fall the trees and haul
out stumps, without horse or oxen to help. Their homestead had
good soil and a year-round spring. "We grew enough to keep two
cows when the children were little, and we sold lots of vegetables
to the logging camps, and lots and lots of fruit. We planted over a
hundred fruit trees—pears, plums, cherries, apples," she told Dawson.[8] The Roos children were among the 57 children in the inlet
remembered by Nancy Crowther.

We then went across the arm to look at a picto which I had
spotted on a cliff face. It turned out to be a good one, but we
decided to run to the head of Okeover Arm to Freke Anchorage and look around there. There was an Indian village of small
shake houses by the stream, such as we see further north, and
there were remains of several fish traps made of boulders. After
lunch we ran back to the picto and I made *Toketie* fast alongside
the bluff and took photos and sketched while Amy fished. We
then ran over to the other side of the arm and picked Ed up and
returned to Thors Cove.

(July 9, 1935)

During the morning we johnsoned to Wootten Bay and viewed
the inlet from the same spot where we were nine years ago. We

went ashore, meeting Mrs. Briskoe, who lives at the head of Wootten Bay and the late Mr. and Mrs. Briskoe's married daughter who lives in the old house in Portage Cove. Their husbands were working in the camp in Theodosia Arm and the wives were glad to have a chat with visitors. These people no doubt feel the solitude, like so many others in the more remote places. They want to sell the old home. The portage from Portage Cove to Wootten Bay is deep midden right across and there must have been quite a settlement here.

(July 10, 1935)

I went up to Ed's cabin and we had a session of crib, finishing up at lunch time with six games apiece, with a skunk each. Amy returned with no fish. Ed came to lunch, which we ate on *Toketie* with her stern end resting on the sandy flat bay as I had anchored a little too far in, and the tides are low now. It was a very hot afternoon and poor little Nannie was overcome, but Amy brought her round by dousing water from the spring on her head. In the evening a young fellow named Thorburn from the logging camp at the mouth of the bay rowed over.

(July 20, 1936)

Ed and I finished up our cribbage championship at noon. We played 89 games since we started a day or two ago, and Ed was 3 games to the good.

(July 23, 1936)

Visited Dick Parker at his logging camp at Trevenon Bay. He insisted on us stopping to dinner. The boiler inspector, Mr. Denham, with his skipper, arrived shortly after we did. The two latter rowed across the bay after dinner, with the two girl cooks from the camp, to look at some Indian graves on the point. We looked at the new cook-house and I took photos of the camp and Parker. Parker does not think camps will be running again till October this dry year.

(July 29, 1938)

Leaving Ed and the cribbage tournament behind, the *Toketie* moved out of Malaspina Inlet and turned northeast up Desolation Sound for a first stop at Mink Island.

We ran to the E. Bay on Mink Id. where we had tea. It is a fine sheltered bay, with a little stream running down the rocks into

the sea, a perfect place to make lily ponds, water gardens, etc.
There was a yawl in the bay from the Royal Vancouver Yacht
Club, and the owner made us welcome to the bay. I could not
gather whether he owned the island, but from what he said he
often goes there. He told us of an ancient pictograph on the
bluff just outside the bay, but it is not easy to make out what it
represents. At 4.45 we left for "Flea Village".

(July 11, 1934)

Prideaux Haven. Anchored under Flea Village. We went ashore
and saw Saulter and his chum Frank who were in the boat
house at work on their 30-foot boat. They have arrived at the
planking stage of construction. Phil Lavigne from the next bay
arrived with some tobacco for Saulter – he had been to Refuge
Cove. After supper I went ashore and played cribbage with
Saulter till 11.30 P.M.

(July 12, 1934)

The Barrows' friends Saulter and Frank lived on the site of a long-
deserted Indian village, built on the top of a steep-sided rocky islet,
the location giving some protection from the raids of slave-hunting
northern tribes. In June 1792, when the two vessels of Captain Vancouver, the *Discovery* and the *Chatham,* and two vessels of Com-
manders Galiano and Valdes, the *Sutil* and the *Mexicana,* were anchored together in Teakerne Arm, a number of British officers and
sailors, exploring in a small open boat, were on shore near the
place where Barrow and Saulter later played cribbage. Suddenly
the British were attacked by "an unexpected numberous enemy."
Archibald Menzies, the surgeon-naturalist with Vancouver, gives
an account of the incident:

> From the fresh appearance of everything about this village &
> the intollerable stench it would seem as if it had been very
> lately occupied by the Natives. The narrow Lanes between the
> Houses were full of filth, nastiness & swarmed with myriad of
> Fleas which fixed themselves on our Shoes, Stockings and
> cloths in such incredible numbers that the whole party was
> obliged to quit the rock in great precipitation, leaving the re-
> mainder of these Assailants in full possession of their Garrison
> without the least desire of facing again such troublesome
> enemy. We no sooner got to the Water side than some imme-
> diately stripped themselves quite naked & immersed their

Cloth, others plunged themselves wholly into the Sea in expectation of drowning their adherents, but to little or no purpose, for after being submerged for some time they leaped about as frisky as ever; in short, we towd some of the Cloths astern of the Boats, but nothing would clear them of this Vermin till in the evening we steeped them in boiling water. This Village from the disasters we met with obtained the name of Flea Village.[9]

Along the Inside Coast the place names frequently remind modern explorers of Vancouver's and the Spanish expeditions. Vancouver vainly hoped to find a passage that would permit him to pass through the mountain mass. Perhaps it was his disappointment, perhaps the foul weather that blew him out of the sound, that led him to give this favourite holiday place the dreary name "Desolation Sound".

To preserve part of this coast for cruising people, a marine park of 22 square miles has been established, with about 40 miles of saltwater shoreline and hiking trails leading to the small lakes.

Head of Melanie Cove: got a nice feed of rhubarb and some sweet williams and honeysuckle which were growing in the much overgrown garden of an old shack. The late occupant greeted people with a shotgun, and he had to be removed. The flowers, which are decorating our cabin table, smell so sweet. We then went to Laura Cove and Phil Lavigne showed us his garden, everything growing well, especially the tobacco plants. He grows his own smoking tobacco. His goats followed us about like dogs. We bought some lettuce, carrots and gooseberries & some goats milk, and he is killing a couple of young roosters for us this evening. He took us to his shack, as tidy and clean as could be. He is over 70 but looks much younger & gets the old age pension, $20 a month. There was a mink on the beach which Rinnie and Nanette tried to catch, but the old man did not want it caught. He watches it every day, and it does not kill his chickens. A good many ravens about here. I went ashore this afternoon and watched Saulter & Frank putting a plank on their boat, a West Coast troller, Model C. (Washington K. D. Boat Co.)

(July 7, 1933)

Saulter and Frank came alongside the boat and gave us a fine lot of peas & potatoes. Also a box full of papers and magazines. Later on they took off one of the battens by one of the windows on the cabin which had sprung away from the panel. Frank Firdette had done some pretty poor work here when he repaired *Toketie* after the shipwreck. However, our friends made a good job, and daylight is no longer visible through the cabin. They have six more planks to put on, all split and hand dressed from cedar they got in the woods. I had a session of cribbage with Saulter in the evening, and then returned to *Toketie*, got under the table and changed plates in my camera.

(July 12, 1934)

Two years later, when the Barrows returned to Flea Village, Saulter and Frank were still working at their boat:

Frank came out with a pan of peas which he had just picked. I went ashore with him and saw the motor-troller, which they hope to finish in a month or two. Amy and I rowed round Roffey Id. before we turned in. Saulter and Frank are busy logging now. They leave at about 5 A.M. and get home about 11, when they spend the rest of the day working on their troller. They are getting it caulked next week. Saulter has his boy and his brother-in-law staying with them, and they are learning the logging business. Next summer Saulter is going to send them off on their own, logging. The price of logs has stayed up this year, and everyone seems busy and contented. There is always the worry, however, of unfair scaling of logs, the possibility of crooked brokers, and the theft of a few boom-chains every time a boom goes to town; but what can a logger do when he is many miles away and has to trust to other people.

(July 23, 1936)

When another two years have passed and the Barrows once again visit their friends, the news of Saulter is not so good:

Anchored in front of Phil Lavigne's. I went up to Phil's and wrote letters for him to his French-Canadian relations in Quebec. They were in answer to letters he had received towards the end of last year. I had to read them to him, and those written in French were easier to read than those written in English. He told us Frank had to take Saulter down to hospital a short

while ago for a second operation. Mr. Easthope told me when
we were at Princess Louisa Inlet that Saulter had just returned
home after an operation.

(July 29, 1938)

Just as we were ready to start at 1.25 I was pulling in the dinghy
rope and did not notice that A. was putting a gas can into it.
The result was that she got a barbed triangle hook from the
plug bait imbedded in her finger. We did not seem to have anything suitable to cut it out so we ran to the logging camp near
Forbes Bay, hoping to be able to use a first aid kit and possibly
get the services of a first aid man. However, there was nothing
to be got there so we hurried off to Refuge Cove. The engine
played up and stopped constantly, lack of gas and some trouble
in the distributor which I was not able to locate. I managed to
get the engine going at about half speed and we were able to get
to Refuge Cove where Jack Tindall cut the hook out after being
in for nearly three hours. Luckily Amy had iodine on board and
she was able to treat it at once after the hook got in.

(August 13, 1941)

Stopped at the entrance of Marylebone Lagoon for lunch. We
seemed to have the sea to ourselves, the only boat we met being
the tug *Queen,* yarding down Waddington Channel. We anchored close to the narrows as I thought someone had told me
they were rocky, but later I found this was not the case, and the
only trouble is that there is not much water at a very low tide.
After lunch we rowed to the head and walked over to the lake,
putting up a covy of grouse on the way. In the afternoon Mr.
Christenson arrived with his small boy and girl. We called on
them later and the children showed us some Indian artifacts
they had found. We tied up for the night to their float and they
came down to see our Indian stuff and have a talk.

(August 1, 1938)

Marylebone Lagoon is a tiny slit at the east side of the entrance to
Waddington Channel. Leaving the lagoon, the *Toketie* turned north
up Waddington Channel and then veered northeast into Pendrell
Sound, the inlet that almost splits East Redonda Island into two
islands.

Went on to where the pictographs are and anchored. Mr.

Heatley came along on his way home from the place where he
is hand-logging, and he stopped for a yarn. The weather got wet
and windy so we went over and made fast to Mr. Heatley's
launch. He is here with two sons, one helping him in the woods
and the other a boy of about 9. Mr. Heatley gave us two loaves
of home-made bread. He had run a bakery in Vancouver until
1915, when he came up here and hand-logged. This job in the
open he much prefers to city life, though he says he does not
know whether it is quite as good for the rest of the family. His
wife and the rest of the children live on a float in Galley Bay,
Gifford Peninsula.

(July 13, 1939)

Galley Bay is near the entrance to Malaspina Inlet, at the eastern
end of Desolation Sound.

We went ashore and talked with the Heatleys after breakfast.
He was baking bread. It cleared up a bit about 11 o'clock and the
rain stopped. After lunch we towed the Heatleys to the place
where they were hand-logging and then went to the bluff
where the pictographs were and photographed and sketched
them which took quite a time. At a quarter of five we left, and
went down the Sound as far as Wood and Armitage's float
where we tied for the night. They invited us to supper and
treated us with much hospitality.

(July 14, 1934)

Our friends [Wood and Armitage] left about 10.30 A.M. in their
launch for Refuge Cove, this being mail day, and we left shortly
after to go to Bliss Landing for mail, but when we got to the
mouth of Pendrell Sound we found a strong southeaster blowing, and both boats returned to the float. Wood and Armitage
came to lunch with us. Rain came down in torrents but just before dark it let up, and the wind increased. We went inside the
boom, and are as comfortable as could be. This is a pretty sheltered spot. Up these inlets one cannot judge what the wind is
doing outside. This morning the wind was blowing down this
part of Pendrell Sound, near the head, and at the mouth it was
blowing up the Sound.

(July 5, 1934)

Still blowing S.E. outside, and rain, so we stayed at the float and enjoyed hot-cake breakfast with our friends and they had lunch with us. We have plenty to eat, lots to read, and a sleep in the afternoon soon passes the day. Wood and Armitage are fine loggers. They have been lucky to get a fair price on their logs and are able to live comfortably, and get what they want. It does one good to see pleasant conditions as this. They were both overseas, Wood in the Canadian Machine Gun Corps and Armitage, an Australian, in the Canadian Railway Corps.

(July 16, 1934)

We had our morning tea as usual, but Armitage called us over to his cabin for hot cakes, which we did not want to pass up. They were tip top and Amy ate nine, but I could not manage quite so many. During the morning Armitage came with us to the head of the Sound. He had papers for Heatley, but not finding him at his cabin we ran over to the pictographs, near where he was logging. We found him there and he came aboard. Amy made a superb instant tapioca pudding and Wood and I had three helpings. Also bottled pears which Ed Berglund gave us, which were excellent.

(July 31, 1938)

Now the Barrows returned to Refuge Cove once more, the shopping and mail centre for Desolation Sound residents. This time Amy had no hook imbedded in her finger and the motor was also in good condition.

Refuge Cove. Went behind the boom. We posted mail, the boat calling here at about 2 A.M. tonight. We had tea with fresh cow's milk, that always being obtainable here and kept on ice down at the float. About midnight Mr. Barnes and his family arrived from Toba Inlet in his gas-boat of quaint naval architecture, looking like a gigantic shoe. The Barnes family did a lot of talking before settling down for the night in their boat close to ours. At 4 A.M. the *Chelohsin* arrived with mail and freight. About 8 A.M. boats began to arrive, the owners coming for the mail and their weekly supplies. Sunday is a busy day for Jack Tindall, the storekeeper. We saw Saulter and Frank, Wood and Armitage, Conner and Scott.

(July 25, 1936)

Jack Tindall said that Spilsbury was in the neighbourhood and

would be in during the afternoon. He short-waved him and
told him I would like to see him. When he arrived I got him to
give the radio a look over, as nothing has been done to it since
we got it. He said the tubes were still O.K. and the noise we get
as we go further north was caused by our aerial being so close
to the water. He rigged up an aerial which I fixed to a 9 ft. pole
over the cabin, a contrivance I can easily take down when we
are running and easily put up. This evening we found a vast im-
provement when we turned on the radio. Spilsbury altered the
band so that now we can get Cape Lazo and tugs. We are inside
the boom and it is quiet and we are comfortable.

(August 2, 1938)

Dick Parker came in on his way to Powell River, to see the doctor. He came over for a chat. He looks very ill and I think has
some kind of heart trouble. He was logging in Toba Inlet but is
going back to Malaspina Inlet where he was before. Mr. Murray
came in at 8 A.M. with his speed-boat from Teakerne Arm and I
asked him about the prospects of getting a movie of breaking
up a raft, but he said they would not be doing that for some
weeks. However, he said they were loading a million feet of
logs on a log hulk and would be finished this evening. I thought
that would make a good shot, but when I tried to start up the
engine, only one cylinder fired, and on investigation I found a
lot of water in the cylinder and plugs. I saw that something was
certainly wrong, and I took off the head and found about half a
cup of water in the aft cylinder and the valves and plugs very
wet. I dried out the parts and later in the day Mr. Kent, the
machinist from Blind Creek, happened to come in to the float
and I got him to take out the valves and dry them and grind
them, as they were not in good shape. We finished the business
about 4.30 and there is nothing to do now but to wait till Sunday or Tuesday, till the new gasket comes. Forrester came in on
his way up to Toba Inlet and I gave him a message for Jim Stapleton to the effect that we would be here till Sunday and as
Monday was registration day, he had better come here to reg-
ister.

(August 13, 1940)

There was not much to do today. There are no roads here so
we could not get a walk except on the float. Sheldon came in

during the evening from Pendrell Sound and we had a chat with him. I played crib and rummy with Jack Parry and his wife till 10.30 P.M.

(August 15, 1940)

The gasket arrived by last night's boat and I got busy putting the head on. Christenson and his son came to speak to us; they had rowed from the Salt Lagoon to Refuge Cove. They had lunch with us. The *John Antle* came in for a short stop and Wally Smith had a look at my engine. I got things together and started up without trouble. However, there was water on the valves after the run, and as I knew the new gasket was tight I took the manifold off and found a fair sized hole in it, and it had evidently been leaking for some time, getting worse and worse. Jack Parry is going to tow us over to Squirrel Cove tomorrow with the UPG and I hope Middleton will be able to weld it. Mr. and Mrs. Jack Tindall showed us their garden, a charming spot, with the creek running through the middle. Jack sometimes in the winter has trouble with too much water which cuts out the banks. The creek operates a Pelton wheel to provide electricity.

(August 18, 1940)

Jack Parry towed us over to Squirrel Cove and I got Middleton busy on the manifold. There were three holes in it, and it was a difficult job to weld. Middleton worked on another job for some time, but at six o'clock we thought all the holes were welded but found a leak still. The raft went up to Teakerne Arm this afternoon, and I hope we shall not be too late to see it bust up.

(August 19, 1940)

Until the invention of the Davis raft in 1913, logs were towed to market in flat booms held together by chains, a perilous method of moving logs. Although the tugboats would take shelter if they had warning of bad weather, all too frequently the booms broke and the logs were scattered, a year's hard-won harvest lost. In a Davis raft the logs were held with wires and chains in bundles about 475 feet long and 30 feet deep, containing about 3,600,000 board feet.

Middleton worked away at the manifold, but it was a pretty hopeless job. We would weld it in one place and there would be a leak in another. About the middle of the morning Brownie

Horth blew in with his family, from Refuge Cove, coming over
to see if he could be of assistance. We decided at noon to run
the engine with the manifold dry. Brown offered to take us to
Teakerne Arm to take a movie of busting up the raft, and Middleton went off to a picnic after lunch. Amy stayed on the *Toketie* but I went off with the Horths to Teakerne Arm where we
found that the raft was to be bust up tomorrow at ten. We went
to the float and met Mr. Kelly of Kelly Raft fame. We returned
to Squirrel Cove.

(August 20, 1940)

Middleton came to the boat to work on the manifold and soon
after Brown arrived and offered to take us to Teakerne Arm.
Amy wished to stay on *Toketie* but I went off. It was an unplea-
sant damp day with rain at intervals. I showed Donna and Allan
my card tricks and Brown, Nellie, Louis and I played four-
handed crib. About 4 P.M. the raft was ready and Brown took us
over close to the boom where we had a good view. Mr. Murray
fired the five charges from the shore and the raft started to
break up and spread out. I was on the roof of the pilot house
under a canvas covering which Brown had kindly rigged up to
keep my camera dry. The light was pretty bum but I shot a lot
of film at F1.5. We got back to Squirrel Cove shortly before six.
Amy and I went up to the Middletons and stayed some time.
They made us stay for tea and Mr. Middleton kept us in fits of
laughter with funny experiences, he being a splendid story
teller.

(August 21, 1940)

Middleton came down to finish the job on our engine and we
got her going again. We then put to sea and the engine ran perfectly. Mr. Middleton took the wheel and broke my steering
rope, for which I was thankful, since I had seen a weak place in
it but foolishly thought it would last us the trip. It was a calm
day and a good spot to rob three turns off the cabin steering
wheel and by doing that we were able to make a splice where
there was nothing to get in the way. We anchored by the float
and had a delayed lunch, afterwards going ashore. Chief Julian
was on his boat and as I wanted to see him, I went over and had
a chat. The time was not suitable for a talk about pictographs,
so I hope to visit him tomorrow at his home. At 4.10 P.M. we
went into the inner harbour through a narrow entrance with

plenty of water and found a perfect sheltered anchorage simply cluttered up with dozens of booms of logs. In fact they were all round the shores, with just a channel in the middle for tugs to bring in more. What would be a delightful anchorage with four to six fathoms all over is nothing more than a storage bay for the Powell River Co. I do not blame the Powell River Co. but the government for allowing such a thing. And yet, I suppose, if I got foreshore rights I could do the same.

(August 22, 1940)

Went to the Indian village in *Toketie* and I went up to see Chief Julian. The poor old chap was lying down as he did not feel very well. His nephew was at the house and I got him to tell Julian not to bother about getting up and talking, but the old fellow got up all the same and I showed him a few of the pictograph sketches and photos. I got a little information but Julian evidently does not know much about the meaning of pictographs. He said there was a man from California here this year getting information from him, I expect ethnological stuff. I cut my visit short as Julian was not feeling too good. He tells me he is 96 which I rather doubt.

(August 23, 1936)

After dinner, boiled rock-cod and dressing, marrow, carrots and potatoes, we ran to the wharf and loaded up with supplies, the *Chelohsin* having called during the night. After getting gas and water and a chat with Mr. Middleton, who we presented with a sketch which Amy and I had done, entitled "And the Lord sent a plague of locusts and flies", we returned to the inner anchorage and had tea.

(August 24, 1941)

Fascinated by machinery, Barrow returned to Teakerne Arm to look at a drag-saw:

I took a photo with the small camera of the 14-foot drag-saw for quartering the enormous spruce logs which come in the rafts. The saw had last cut a spruce 7 feet wide, but one of the men told me they often get spruce logs over eight feet in diameter. The gangways to the float were nice eight-foot planks, and floating. There was hardly a trickle over the waterfall and they are short of water at the camp.

(September 6, 1938)

In June 1792 Menzies described this same waterfall in early summer: "a beautiful Waterfall which issued from a Lake close behind
it & precipitated a wide foaming stream into the Sea over a shelving
rock precipice of about thirty yards high; its wild romantic appearance aided by its rugged situation & the gloomy forests which
surrounded it, rendered it a place of resort for small parties to visit
during our stay. And in the Lake itself we found some Bivalve Shells
which were quite new to me."[10]

> The *Monongahela* passed by this morning with, as I found out
> after, a million four thousand feet of logs on board, most of the
> logs being high grade spruce for aeroplanes. We passed along
> the south shore of Teakerne Arm looking for a pictograph,
> which we did not find, and I took a movie of the *Monongahela*
> just after the *Marmion* left her. They soon started putting logs
> overboard from both ends of the vessel and I got busy taking
> movies of the proceedings. After quitting time we had a chat
> with one of the men off the barge and he told us they would
> have the barge unloaded by evening tomorrow, which seems
> pretty quick work. We are tied up to the camp float for the
> night.
>
> (August 22, 1940)

The *Monongahela* was originally the 211-foot *Balasore*, built in Scotland in 1892. Sold to a German firm, then captured during the First
World War and interned at Astoria on the Columbia River, she was
bought in 1936 by the Kelly Logging Company and converted to a
log-carrying barge, one of the first on the Pacific coast.

Departing from Desolation Sound, the *Toketie* turned southward,
stopped at Squirrel Cove, then rounded Mary Point on the southeast corner of Cortes Island and entered Cortes Bay, finally finding
a safe anchorage in a corner of the bay known as Blind Creek.

> After getting some supplies we left Squirrel Cove for Blind
> Creek, where we anchored for the night. We went ashore &
> saw some people named Roark living close to where we are an-
> chored. They showed us their garden & gave us some radishes.
> They said they had a very hard time last winter but did not get
> any relief although they applied for it. They have not bought
> any clothes for 5 years but Mrs. Roark showed us cushions she
> had made out of gunny sacks & designs worked on them in old

coloured wool. She had made lovely rugs out of old coloured rags, a coat for her husband out of gunny sacks, and a splendid hat for herself out of a flour sack. Also a couple of young roosters & some eggs completed our purchases. She had been a school teacher before she married, and her husband has been cook in a logging camp. Before that Roark was a cattle puncher in Texas. Originally from Belfast.

(July 9, 1933)

Rain, and a strong south-easter blowing. We went ashore in the morning and I played cribbage with Mrs. Roark. She plays the piano very well & used to teach. After lunch we walked to Mr. John Manson's, 4 miles away, as I thought he would be able to tell us something about the Indian fortifications in Gorge Harbour. He did not know anything about it, but told me to see Mr. Allan there. He told us, however, of a petroglyph between the old Indian village, Paukeanum, near Smelt Bay & Manson's Landing. Also, one on the south end of Mary Id. The dogs put up a lot of grouse on our walk.

(July 10, 1933)

John Manson ought to have heard stories about the Indian fortifications, for he came to Cortes Island in 1890 to join his brother Michael, the first white settler, who had arrived in 1888. Michael had married Jane Renwick of Nanaimo in a romantic elopement and John came to help them run a trading post. From the Indians they got dogfish oil, which they sold to the coal mines in Nanaimo as lubricating oil at 37½¢ a gallon; bear gall which was sold as a medicine to the Chinese miners in Nanaimo; deer horns which retailed at 25¢, 50¢ or 75¢ a set, depending on size; mink skins (50¢), coon skins (25¢) and marten skins (one dollar). For the most part they maintained friendly relationships with their Indian trading partners, Michael gaining experience which later made him an excellent justice of the peace.

John was only 19 when he joined Michael on Cortes Island. After the Biblical seven years of hard labour, he returned to the Shetlands to marry his childhood sweetheart, Margaret Ellen Smith, and to bring her to his Canadian island. John did an amazing amount of rowing in those years, rowing his butchered beef and mutton down to Comox, rowing to Mitlenatch Island where he kept sheep, rowing orders to the logging camps. Doris Andersen in

Evergreen Islands relates that once he rowed 200 miles, to the head of Knight Inlet and back, just to fetch two school girls to board at the Mansons' home, to bring the number of pupils up to the number required for a school.

In his older days, when the Barrows visited him, John Manson, known to the Cortes Islanders as "Uncle John", grew fine crops of potatoes, and with the help of his collie, Jock, looked after a flock of sheep. He loved to beachcomb. Even in his eighties he would row close to the shoreline of Cortes Island to see what the sea had brought.

In 1973 the Parks Branch of the British Columbia government purchased 117 acres at Manson's Landing for a provincial park, including the dock area with its fine sand beach and the entire peninsula between ocean and lake.

> Went ashore and met Captain Finnie who has a place just by our anchorage. He went to war when he was 18 and was in the Flying Corps in Egypt and India. He crashed and was taken prisoner by the Afghans and was very well treated. He was a prisoner in Germany also for a short time. He came out to Canada in 1921 & was in the Flying Corps here. He crashed near Calgary & was badly damaged. He is slowly regaining his health on Cortes Id. & is fixing up his property here, which gives him a lot of pleasure.
>
> (July 11, 1933)

> Moved to Gorge Harbour. Met Mr. Pool on the float. He came aboard and had a yarn. He said the Haidas were enticed to the Gorge by the local Indians for a conference & large boulders from above were dropped on them. The marks on the bluff in red oxide are supposed to be the score of those they bumped off, but I am doubtful about this. We went over to Paukeanam & spotted a big petroglyph of a killer whale on a big granite boulder near by. Went over to Mary Id. and hunted along the beach for more than a mile for the petroglyph but did not find it.
>
> (July 18, 1933)

The Mr. Pool whom Francis Barrow encountered on the Gorge Harbour float is described in *The Protected Place* by Gilean Douglas, who not only inhabits the Pool house but also caught a ghostly glimpse of Mr. Pool in the garden. John Pool and his dainty wife, Elizabeth, went from York in England to Liverpool, on to Boporo in Sierra Leone where he served as school inspector, then to Qualicum Beach and finally to Cortes Island. When the First World War was declared, John served in the Army Medical Corps. Returning to Cortes, he built the house facing Marina Island, which Cortes people call Mary Island ("Don't hug Mary too close", they advise yachtsmen who go through this pass). Elizabeth and John made this wild place bloom like an English garden. John sent specimens of the local wild plants to the Provincial Museum. Gilean Douglas quotes a Cortes neighbour as saying that listening to John Pool and Bernie Allen discoursing on a flower was "like a mental minuet".

Gilean Douglas wished she could have talked with John Pool about the place they both loved, but John had been dead for ten years when Gilean came to Cortes Island. Shortly after her arrival she asked a neighbour what John Pool looked like and was told that he was tall, thin and fair. One day she looked out her window and saw a medium-tall, medium-built man with brown hair wearing striped coveralls coming up the path. She went to open the back door to welcome the stranger but there was no one there. She searched all around but found no one. Shortly after this odd episode she was chatting with a Cortes Islander:

"Your description of John Pool in that article wasn't quite right," he said.

"Why, what did he look like?"

"Medium height, average build, brown hair ... I remember he used to wear black and white striped overalls a lot."[11]

John and Elizabeth Pool's garden is still tended and loved by Gilean Douglas.

> Went to the south end of Gorge Harbour in the row boat and had lunch at Gorge Harbour Lodge, run by Mrs. Corneille. It is a nice place, and here I met Mr. Bernard Allan who gave me the legend about dropping boulders on the heads of hostile Indians as told by Chief George of Church House in 1895.
>
> (July 14, 1933)

> Met Mr. Breeze and tied up to his mooring. Mr. Breeze came with us about a mile up the coast and I took photos and sketched an interesting pictograph which we had not seen before. It was

a lovely day. When we got back I finished sketching the pictographs in the gorge at Gorge Harbour.

(July 18, 1934)

In the morning Mr. Breeze took us up to a place under the bluff at the back of his house where there are overhanging rocks forming caves where the Indians many years ago buried their dead, often after a smallpox outbreak. We found many bones, and bits of cedar coffin-boxes, and bits of cedar mat, but the place has been raided so often by curio hunters that there is nothing of any interest left. In the afternoon we went to Whaletown, Mr. Breeze accompanying us, and after posting mail and getting bread, we went to the west side of Mary Id., hoping to make a landing at an old Indian village site there. However, as there are a lot of boulders near the shore, and they are hard to see except on a sunny day when the water is clear, we decided to give it a miss and returned to the spot at the north end of Mary Id. where I took the photo of the pictograph. We found another and I made a sketch.

(July 20, 1934)

Soon after breakfast we received a visit from Percy Belsen, but we were sorry he could only stay for a short time. He invited us to go up to the camp, and he is calling for us tomorrow by car at the wharf at 4.30 P.M. A little later who should come in but Cam Layard and Mr. Head from Cowichan Bay, in his boat *Dido*. They had just come down from Philipps Arm. They did not stay very long, and were on their way to Seymour Narrows. Mr. Breeze came to lunch with us. He took us to the top of the Gorge at the back of his place. It is a wonderful spot and must have been occupied by many Indians in early times, and would have been a pretty difficult spot to attack, a steep slope being the only approach to the top, and sheer cliffs all round the other part.

(July 22, 1934)

At 4.30 Percy arrived with the truck. We left for the logging camp about 8 miles away at the back of Carrington Bay, and found Bill Horth, Frank Norris and Shepheard, from Salt Spring Id., quite a North Saanich gathering. They are living in a nice old house, covered with honeysuckle, and a Mrs. Alloway and her son look after the feeding. We had a fine supper on our arrival, and talked of North Saanich news. There is a lake at the back of the house, and fine trout in it; they were rising to beat the band. The boys are cutting fine fir, and the sticks are pretty big. They have a 60 H.P. tractor to haul out the logs. Percy drove us back, and on the way we looked at the place where they skid the logs down into the salt lagoon which joins Carrington Bay. Percy and Shepheard came on board and listened to the "Province" news. It was just 8.15 when they returned to the camp and we to Mr. Breeze's mooring.

(July 23, 1934)

A very hot summer day. In the afternoon Amy made apple jelly for Mr. Breeze and he and I went into Gorge Harbour where Mr. B. keeps his launch, and he tried to make the engine go after a year of idleness. His efforts were not very successful.

(July 24, 1934)

When they were very young, Ned Breeze and his wife left Vancouver in a 12-foot rowboat, with no particular destination in mind except that they were determined not to return to the city. Born in Peterborough, Ontario, Ned had lived in New York and Montana. Looking for the place they would call home, they rowed northwards at a leisurely pace, camping on the beaches, sheltered by a piece of tarpaulin when it rained. They had some food in a wooden box and fishing poles jutted out at the prow. They searched in this fashion for most of a summer and their rowing finally brought them to Marina Island, close to Cortes, where a fox farm was being established. While working for the fox farm owner, Ned was sent on errands to Gorge Harbour, and there he found the site for their log house, near the harbour's narrow, steep-sided entrance. He and his wife planted the rock terraces with lilies and wild snapdragon. A short trail meandered from the house to a long lagoon with a sandy bottom. A fine spring of fresh water gushed from the rock nearby. Ned supported his family by working summers in fish canneries or on survey parties. He had only one daughter, famous for regularly swimming out to meet the steamer, to collect the mail. In the days before the First World War, when there were many remittance men and settlers, the social life on Cortes Island was lively indeed, and the Breeze house was renowned for its excellent library.

Once he could tackle the tide rips in his canoe, or cut three cords
of wood in a day, but when the Barrows knew Ned Breeze he was
old, his wife and daughter dead. The *Sun* newspaper reporter who
interviewed him in 1948, the year of his death at the age of 80, reported that he refused to leave his old home because "an enormous
collection of cats and two amazingly fat dogs depended on him for
support."

"Fishing is no longer the simple matter it was," he remarked.
"The fish are both fewer and fussier."[12]

Spending their last Cortes night in the harbour at Whaletown,
the Barrows had an early morning exchange with a road-map
yachtsman:

> Last evening a big sailing yacht from Seattle came in and they
> anchored near the head of the bay. This morning she was hard
> and fast by the stern with the rudder half out of water. While I
> was cooking breakfast a young fellow from the yacht came to
> the float and asked me when was low water. I asked him if he
> had a Canadian tide table which he had, but he said the infor-
> mation was not in it. I assured him it was and found that it was
> then the turn of the tide. He did not seem to believe me and
> went off to ask someone else. When he came back I suggested
> that they might have sounded before anchoring.
>
> (August 17, 1941)

Now the *Toketie* motored westward, leaving Cortes Island in her
wake, with a first stop at Heriot Bay on Quadra Island.

> At the store I met W. Law, a fisherman who told me of a petro-
> glyph near the end of Cape Mudge, on the east side. Mr. Law is
> interested in Indian things and he was a lucky find. He was
> overseas and saw much carnage. He took his boat and we ours
> to his parents home in Hyacinthe Bay. They welcomed us and
> insisted on us staying to supper. Mr. Law Sr. knew Dr. New-
> combe when he was among the Queen Charlotte Islands in
> 1900. We returned to our anchorage near the wharf and close
> by the old *I'llaway*.
>
> (July 26, 1934)

William Law and his wife and children came from New Zealand
to Hyacinthe Bay, Quadra Island, in 1909, where they bought land
which had been logged by Hiram McCormack. They converted

McCormack's two-storey store and warehouse into the spacious home in which Francis and Amy Barrow were entertained. To attend school, the young Laws hiked a narrow trail which twisted and looped round coves and headlands to Heriot Bay. When Bill Law Jr. returned from the horrors of the war to the serenity of Hyacinthe Bay, he worked first for the old Goss Packing Company, then for B.C. Packers, before becoming a patrol officer for the Department of Fisheries. Hiding behind a pen name, "The Deckhand", he drew cartoons and wrote a column for *The Fisherman*. One of the people he wrote about was his friend Matt Gerrard, whom the Barrows now visited in Heriot Bay.

> Made fast to the Heriot Bay wharf. After supper we started off to see Mrs. Gerrard and Dorris and met them coming down to see us. We returned to Dorris's house and after a cup of tea they came down to the boat.
>
> (September 4, 1940)

One column from "The Deckhand" was headlined "Old Timer Only Took Union Fish". Bill Law explained that Matt Gerrard, an electrician in the city, had decided to be a fisherman in 1920, then changed his mind and bought Stuart Island Landing instead. Here he built a store, house and floats, established a gas station and became a fish buyer. When the Pacific Coast Fishermen's Union was formed, he was a dedicated member, hoping for a better deal for the fishermen he knew so well. Perhaps his was the first closed shop in a primary industry in British Columbia, for he put P.C.F.U. in huge letters on the roof of his ice house, and bought only union fish. Later the Gerrards lived at Heriot Bay, where the Barrows photographed them.

> We went up to see Mrs. Gerrard and Dorris in the morning and had lunch with them. In the afternoon we got Mr. Caldwell to take us for a drive in his car to Quathiaski Cove where I took movies while the others were having ice-cream at the store. We came back by Drew Harbour. I had a yarn with Mr. Caldwell at his store, about Victoria and North Saanich, he having been with Bray in the old days. Mrs. Gerrard, Dorris and Dell came to supper on the boat, and Dorris's husband, who is on a seine boat, turned up after.
>
> (September 5, 1940)

In the morning we hired a car and were driven to Cape Mudge, and on the east side, about ¼ miles from the end, I took photos of a petroglyph on a granite boulder.

(July 27, 1934)

We went ashore and saw Mr. Crompton the postmaster, who very kindly made my watch go again, it having stopped coming across from Whaletown. Mr. Crompton used to be with Clayton in Victoria and I have often seen him before today, when he was with Clayton and afterwards with Martin.

(August 17, 1941)

Doris Andersen's history *Evergreen Islands* describes the Union Steamship vessel giving an ear-piercing signal at two o'clock in the morning, as she circled to come in to the Heriot Bay wharf. The sound caused postmaster Edgar Crompton to leap from his bed, pull on clothes and hurry in the dark across the pebbly beach to the wharf, carrying the two sacks of outgoing mail. Crompton, who had spent 16 years in Alaska, trapping, trading and goldmining, was postmaster in Heriot Bay for over a decade. He was also Doris Andersen's father.

The Gerrards came to supper with us and about 7.30 I rowed Amy and Mrs. Gerrard round to the Dickies and we spent the evening with them.

(August 18, 1941)

Probably the Dickies told the Barrows about the terrible fire which almost demolished the house in which they talked. Nothing has been said in the journals about the coast dwellers' fear of forest fires, but Francis Dickie has left a vivid description of this particular fire in 1925, quoted by writer Ruth McVeigh:

"A booming roar out of the west aroused me. May I never hear its like again. I ran up the nearest moss-covered ridge and looked toward the fast approaching sound. I saw miles of heavily timbered rocky slopes aflame. Along a five-mile front swept a wall of flame and rust-coloured smoke. It moved fast, mingling weirdly with the green ranks of the fir. In front of the writhing flames flew an advance guard of flaming twigs and bits of branches, streamers of flame to ignite far ahead the crowns of the trees. A light north wind was increasing and there was the awful suction of fire creating a hurricane of its own. Even with all my possessions in its path, I was held there, awed by this vision of an earthly hell, destroying in a minute what had required a thousand years to grow. From the tops of the flaming timber vast clouds rolled to the sky, becoming strangely white against the clearest of blue. The sun was a blurred red disk. Over moss, rock, trees and even the sea, there lay an other-worldly bluish grey light, in which the evergreens seemingly turned pale as though aware of their inescapable doom. . . . Ahead of the fire deer bounded at speeds varying according to how far they had run. . . . Hundreds of grouse and smaller birds flew low over me, making for a tiny rock island a hundred yards out to sea. Here and there squirrels scolded defiant, until they were shrivelled."[13]

In *Evergreen Islands,* Doris Andersen adds that Francis and Suzanne Dickie, seeing the flames heading directly for their newly-built home, fled down the steep, rocky cliff to their rowboat and there discovered that they had salvaged "the cats, an Airedale dog, bookshelves, a dictionary stand and several washtubs filled with books."[14] Just at this moment, the Columbia Coast Mission boat *Rendezvous* appeared, with Alan Greene at the wheel and the Department of Forestry raft in tow. The raft was equipped with pressure pumps and a hose, which were immediately put to use, spraying the underbrush and trees around the Dickies' house with sea water. This serendipitous cooperation of church and state saved the house.

The man who wrote the vivid description of the fire and who rescued a dictionary stand instead of the family silver, was in fact an author. Born in Carberry, Manitoba, in 1890, Francis Dickie learned from Ernest Thompson Seton in person to love and observe the wilderness world. At 16 he joined a Canadian Pacific Railway survey party, seeking out-of-doors freedom rather than a schoolroom. Three years later he travelled to British Columbia and California, recording his experiences in *Strange Soul's Journeyings.* First a *Calgary Herald* reporter, then an editor in Edmonton, he next married a Parisienne, Suzanne Garnier, and moved to Toronto. Returning to the west the Dickies bought the Heriot Bay house, where they experienced the fire of 1925. In the following year, Francis was sent by the Vancouver *Daily Province* to France, as their correspondent. The Dickies became friends of Somerset Maugham, with whom Francis had a 30-year correspondence, many of the letters discussing gardens.

In 1932 Francis and Suzanne Dickie returned to their house on the rocks at Heriot Bay, where the Barrows visited them in 1941. Interviewing Francis Dickie there in 1974, two years before his death at 86, Ruth McVeigh sat with him in the book-lined study, warmed by a driftwood fire, and distracted by the lovely views of sea, shore and mountains. Dickie's library, which Barrow admired, contained all 32 of Maugham's first editions, later willed to a Victoria library. His collected papers are in the Provincial Archives of British Columbia. Dickie published 150 short stories and countless newspaper and magazine articles; his most successful novel was *The Master Breed*, written in 1949.

To the Dickies and I had a look at his boat which was leaking rather badly. After lunch with the Dickies and a rubber of cribbage, and listening to the B.B.C. news, we returned to the float, and Lorne Le Duke, Mrs. Gerrard's nephew, came down. He and I got busy on my engine as it stopped when the spark was advanced again today. Lorne works in a shop in Vancouver where they overhaul outboard motors. We examined the distributor and found the carbon in the cap a good deal worn. At my suggestion, Lorne took the carbon out of a flashlight battery and filed it down to the size of the distributor, but left it twice as long, and it made much better contact. However, this did not cure the trouble, but it improved it. I got Lorne to change the new condenser for the old one and the engine ran perfectly. I hope it will continue to do so. He stayed to supper with us.

(August 20, 1941)

Mrs. Gerrard came to dinner with us and brought us a box of all sorts of good things to eat. Mr. and Mrs. Crompton came to tea and before we had finished, Francis Dickie arrived with some of his writing for me to read. At 5.00 P.M. we left our kind friends, Mrs. Crompton bringing us down some home-made bread just before we cast off. We were going to run north, but when I slowed down and then advanced the spark again, the engine died on me, so we did not cure the defect after all. We had better go and see Mr. Middleton again.

(August 21, 1941)

But first the Barrows went to Village Bay, just north of Heriot Bay.

> Village Bay, where there is a circle of large stones placed there long ago by the Indians for some ceremony or other. We could not find it.
>
> (September 6, 1934)

> We have traced the ghastly smell in the boat to something in the bilge under the engine, so I took up the floor boards and got all the water and grease and everything out, finishing by wiping over the bilge with rags soaked in gasoline. The smell is better but it has not quite gone. Anyway, I can't do any more. Amy went ashore while I was busy, to look for the circle of stones and she got lost at the lake. Finding her way back she bruised her hip and knees painfully, as her shoes gave out and she had some falls. In the afternoon I went in search of the circle of stones, and after covering a good bit of country, I was unable to find it.
>
> (September 7, 1934)

> Amy put me ashore with cameras and I went in search of the stone circle. With the help of Law's photo I found it after about an hour, and took photos. It was boiling hot packing the cameras and tripod over the fallen timber and up the hill but I was lucky enough to find some huckleberries which eased my thirst. I put up grouse and pigeons on my way but saw no deer. The devils club along the trail to the lake was a tremendous size. I don't remember seeing it in flower before.
>
> (July 11, 1935)

Barrow's photo and notes about this stone circle are the only records existing of this site, which cannot now be found. Stones arranged in somewhat similar circular formations are known from a mountain top near Pender Harbour, where ethnographic records connect them with female puberty ceremonies. Although Barrow made inquiries about the meaning of the stone circles and the rock art, no answers were recorded in his journals. From the work of Boas and others, something is known of the role of art in the Indian cultures of the coast. The reader is referred to the work of Doris Lundy and Beth Hill, listed in the sources.

Back to Cortes Island went the Barrows, seeking the long-suffering Mr. Middleton. When the *Toketie* was running well again, the warmer airs of the Strait of Georgia, the territory of the Coast Salish people, were left behind. To the north lay the close-packed islands and moister climate of the Kwakiutl people. An emptier land awaited *Toketie*.

CHAPTER FIVE

Heading north up Hoskyn Channel between Quadra and Read Islands, approaching Surge Narrows, the *Toketie* departed from the land of Garry oaks and seductive arbutus, flowering dogwood and stands of red alder in the logged-off areas. Northwards lies a region of heavier rainfall, with thick forests of Douglas fir, Sitka spruce, hemlock and red cedar, where a jungle undergrowth of salal, red huckleberry, devil's club and salmonberry grows in such rank profusion that the forests are impenetrable, the cedar boughs sweeping down to touch the sea. In this region the houses are often on log floats, fastened by cables to the trees on the shore.

Living on the jig-saw islands north of the Strait of Georgia has another disadvantage: the tide rips and rapids are more dangerous there. The tide enters the strait through both north and south openings, but the narrower convoluted passages at the north constrict the flow. Thus the difference between high and low tide levels near Victoria is only 5.7 feet, whereas in the channels in the north it is 11.2 feet. Often the little *Toketie* had to wait for slack tide before proceeding.

We ran on as far as the Government float at Surge Narrows and saw Mr. Frost at his store.

(August 4, 1939)

We went over at slack water to retrieve the jigger we lost in Surge Narrows yesterday but we were unsuccessful. It has blown hard from the west all day, but we are nicely sheltered behind the float. I got a STORE sign ready for Frost to paint in the afternoon.

(August 5, 1939)

Frost came to lunch with us and about 1 o'clock the *Chelohsin* arrived. We met Mr. Tipton and Mrs. Dennis and her family, the usual gathering at the weekly boat. Just before we left at 2 P.M. Frost asked us to take a fellow named Monroe with us as far as the Dusenburys, where we were going. It seemed this fellow was going to a small camp nearby as donkeyman. The boys had not met him at Surge Narrows. When we got to the Dusenbury's, Mr. D. said the camp was about half a mile away in Waiatt Bay, so I rowed Monroe to the place and when we got there we found everyone away. They had gone to a picnic at Owen Bay so we rowed back to Bodega Anchorage and went ashore at Mr. Dusenbury's float and up to his store. It is an unbelievable sort of place. The idea of selling us anything was the last thing they wanted, but Mr. and Mrs. Dusenbury ushered us into their living quarters at the back of the store for a talk, which was what they wanted. Dusenbury, whose brother we met at Pender Harbour, used to live in Saanich years ago, stevedoring in Victoria and trapping around Saanich and the islands. He knew Billy Munro of James Id. He said he was trapping on Darcy Id. once and had a yarn with the Chinks there, not knowing they were lepers but he thought they were odd-looking guys as one had no eye lids. We left at 4.10 P.M. and anchored in front of the old Indian village site in Waiatt Bay. There is quite an extensive house site and deep midden all round the horse-shoe bay. At 8 P.M. we left for Owen Bay where we deposited Mr.

Monroe. There were quite a lot of boats there for the movie show and picnic, and we saw the people from San Francisco again, but had not time to talk to them as it was getting dark and we wanted to get back before the rapids started to run.

(August 6, 1939)

Among the folk gathered on the Surge Narrows dock, waiting for the *Chelohsin*, was Robert Tipton, from the west side of Read Island, farmer, storekeeper and justice of the peace. Needing a school for Read Island after he and his wife Ethel had adopted their two nephews and a niece in 1925, he inserted a notice in a Vancouver newspaper offering to help locate pre-emptions on the island for settlers with children. Letters came in response from many parts of the province, all expressing that deep longing for an escape from drab, unrewarding work to an island paradise. However, the reality of island life required more skill, courage and dogged persistence than most of the applicants possessed.

We hit a submerged propeller inspector near White Rock passage, but we never had a sight of it. On arriving at Surge Narrows we made fast behind the boom and Mr. Frost came down. Mr. Montgomery, the Professor, was there too. Frost and the Professor played crib with me on board. We all went into Surge Narrows at slack water on *Toketie* to visit Mr. Heinbokel, who showed us his place and gave us some vegetables. He had an Indian round stone of the target category.

(August 27, 1941)

We left at 11.15 A.M. in order to catch slack water at the Hole-in-the-wall, but when we were a short distance inside Okisollo Channel I saw someone signalling to us from the shore, and going up to them I found two of our friends from the *B.C. Forester* who had been timber cruising, and they had got down to the bottom of a steep bluff and could not get any further. We took them on board and went on about half a mile to the next bay where the *B.C. Forester* was made fast to the boom at a camp. The *B.C. Forester* went on to Klein's camp about a mile further on and we soon joined her, as the Kleins were hauling logs with the cat and a bummer. I took some movies of this job.

(August 27, 1938)

I took a movie of the Store and the Dusenbury's and trust it will be O.K. for there are few stores like it these modern times. Traps, old stable lanterns, coffee grinder of the Victorian era, and a cardboard top-hat box from London among some of the items. Amy was taken off to be told about boils on bottoms and abscesses and such like pleasantries.

(August 5, 1939)

It was frightfully hot and we kept quiet on board. Amy found it so hot that she lay on her bunk reading, her only clothing being a pair of spectacles. At 2 P.M. we started off to have another hunt for the picto near Etta Point, but could not find it. Down Hoskyn Inlet where we hunted for two pictos said to be there. After tea we found one and I made a sketch and took photos.

(July 13, 1935)

As we got into Discovery Passage a school of blackfish showed up. Soon after the *Cardena* and *Venture* passed on their way to Vancouver and I got a shot of both on the one film. A little later we passed through a bunch of seine boats and as one was hauling in we stopped and I got some movies. A good many more fish, humps, than in my film last year. They gave us one and I gave them a packet of cigarettes. Amy boiled the hump and it was first rate, with onions and potatoes.

(August 7, 1939)

The "hump" Amy boiled is a pink or humpback salmon, so named because of the swelling which the male fish develops before spawning.

The *Toketie* had come around the north end of Quadra Island and now turned into Kanish Bay, opening off Discovery Passage, at the north end of Quadra Island.

It was a glorious summer day. We went right up to the head of the bay through a narrow channel and were surprised to find quite a settlement with post and telegraph office, store, government float at which the *Chelohsin* calls, logging camp, and a road which, I believe, leads out of the settlement for six miles. The place is known as Granite Bay and not Kanish Bay. We walked ashore after lunch and visited the store. Mr. and Mrs. Twidle, who run the store, asked us into the house and gave us a very nice afternoon tea. Twidle used to take photos professionally up the coast and he showed me his cameras, all of English make. He has a Thornton Pickard Cine camera with Callmeyer lens which interested me. The Twidles gave us some nice runner beans. We notice the vile smell in the boat that has appeared other times, and which I think must be old engine oil in the bilge.

(August 19, 1936)

There is an old Indian house site here about 300 yards long, shaped like a horse-shoe, and a flat single house site considerably above the other but on the same site. It started to blow quite hard so we turned into the lagoon, about a mile long, and anchored a few hundred yards from the head. The entrance is quite narrow, and it states on the chart there is a depth of 3½ fathoms here, sandy bottom I am glad to say, as the wind is blowing very hard indeed outside, and even in here there are great gusts. There is deep midden on some of the beaches and some house sites.

(August 20, 1936)

The wind blew itself out during the night and after breakfast we visited the middens which have been messed up with the usual old junk and chaos of logging camps. Left for Granite Bay. I bought Twidle's Thornton Pickard Cine camera, which seems to be just what I had been looking for. Twidle has run the store here since 1911. Mrs. Twidle gave us two loaves of home-made bread.

(August 21, 1936)

When Henry Twidle died, aged 77, in April 1956, *The Campbell River Courier* published a brief obituary. He had come to the coast in 1904, working first as timekeeper for the old Hastings Timber Company at Rock Bay. After marrying Agnes Lucy of Toronto in 1907, he took his bride to Granite Bay where they bought the store and hotel opened by Joseph Dick the previous year. Here they stayed for 40 years. He was Granite Bay's first school secretary and also served as stipendiary magistrate. He could not have parted with his movie camera to a more enthusiastic amateur photographer.

Deciding to visit their friend Jim Stapleton at his Toba Inlet camp, the Barrows went back through Okisollo Channel and through Hole-in-the-Wall into Calm Channel and Pryce Channel.

Then on up Toba Inlet and we found three groups of pictos on the way. The wind chased us up the inlet and we were pleased to discover Stapleton's splendid little sheltered bay where we made fast alongside his boat about 10 feet from the shore in very deep water. After supper we went to call on Stapleton and found the Fishery Warden, Mr. Mann, there. They returned to *Toketie* with us and we talked until 1 A.M. Mr. Mann is from Dublin.

(August 17, 1935)

Mann came to lunch with us, and afterwards we went to the head of Toba Inlet, stopping to take two groups of pictos on the way. We all went ashore and saw Mr. Barnes, his Indian wife, and Annie Hill, a jolly wizened-up little old Indian woman. From what Barnes (Junior) has told me at the village of Old Vancouver, there are interesting things to be seen at the head, and as far as I could make out, a boulder painted with old white pigment on the flats; but we saw nothing although Annie was going to take us to her home to show us a stone axe she had found. However, they kept leading us on, and as we did not know how far up the flats her house might be, we decided to return in the rowboat to *Toketie*.

(August 18, 1935)

A bright hot day with a westerly wind. This is a nice cool place, but flies, no-see-ums, bulldog and other varieties are somewhat plentiful, worrying Amy, but leaving me, a tough old bird, alone. We all went up to the head of the Inlet in *Toketie*. On the way the engine suddenly stopped. It took me some time to discover the trouble, which I found to be a broken spring on the timer. Fortunately I had a spare one, and after fixing this and cleaning the strainer on the carburettor, and freeing the Bendix which has stuck, the engine proceeded to run again. We anchored *Toketie* at the edge of the flats and rowed to the bluff near Annie Hill's home up the slough. We found the small pictograph which Joe Barnes had told me about.

(August 5, 1938)

We are waiting for the return of some Indians from Powell River as Stapleton has some groceries for them. He is going to take us up Toba River to the Champion's old place, about 12 miles up. They have now left and there is nobody up the river now.

(August 6, 1938)

Earlier the Barrows had met and photographed the Champions, who had invited the Barrows to visit them at their Toba River homestead. Barrow had been loath to leave *Toketie* at the river mouth.

This is a typical river mouth, lots of snags, deadheads, sandbars, shoal water, and without warning, very deep water. Added to this, the water is like milk and one can see nothing in it. This is not a very good place to anchor as the river silt buries the anchor and if a boat is left for some days, the anchor may be feet down in the mud. But the Champions wanted us very much to return with them up the river. They have few visitors, the last about four years ago. In the event of a universal war and disruption, a place like the Champion's seems the logical spot to retire to, where nature provides so much for man's needs. The fly in the ointment seems to be getting frozen in for three or four months in the winter.

(July 30, 1936)

Two years later, when the Barrows went up the Toba River with Jim Stapleton, the Champions were gone.

When we had had tea in the afternoon, we left for the river. We went up in Champion's boat, which he used when he lived at his place about eight miles up. We had trouble with the engine till we got to the river mouth, where we stopped to see what was the trouble. We had already cleaned out a lot of filth from the gas line. The whole engine was in a hay wire condition, leaking joints fixed up with wood plugs, and rag, wire and string to hold it together. We found the spark plug was defective and when we replaced it with another we had no further trouble for the rest of the trip. The open boat, with a cedar canopy which we found much in the way when we had to pole, Champion has used for a number of years to go up and down the river, and she is a very useful craft for that kind of work, since it is easy to shove her over a bar when one gets stuck. We got up to the Champion ranch just as it got dark, having taken about 4½ hours to make the trip. We did not stick on any sand bar though near the river mouth we skidded for some way over one, but the engine kept going and pulled us off. It is really surprising how well this hay-wire boat and engine behave, in the river. We ran into the bank and packed our stuff up to a cabin where Champion's father and mother used to live. There was a stove in it and we soon had a good supper which we were all ready for. We brought in some oat hay and made up our sleeping quarters on the floor and passed a very comfortable night. We took up a spray gun and fly-tox so that biting insects did not get in their dirty work.

(August 8, 1938)

We got up early and looked round the place. We went for several walks and saw tracks of bear, coon and deer.

(August 9, 1938)

We got up early and started off up the river further and reached Calamity Bay about 10.30. I took a movie of the very high waterfall on the north side of the river. Jim estimated it to be 2000 feet high, and I think it is all of that. We left to go down the river at 4.15 P.M. The mist was rising from it in some of the reaches, which made it hard to see the sand bars. We stuck on the bar near the mouth, but a little poling soon put us off.

(August 30, 1940)

I put up some shelves for Jim in the house on the float to which we are made fast. In the evening I arranged the canned goods on the shelves so that his customers can see what he has to sell. In the afternoon Jim came up with us to the inlet opposite Black's camp and I took some movies of Billy Williams hauling in his gill net, after which the camera refused to work. Billy Williams fixed up his fish well so that I could open the camera in the dark, but after struggling for some time in the fishy atmosphere, I was unable to remedy the trouble so came up to daylight and fresh air. The afternoon I spent making price tickets for the goods in Jim's store. Jim hauled up the prawn net in which there were a dozen nice prawns, but some others had evidently got out through a hole in the top of the trap. Amy cut Jim's hair and we had supper with him. Then I got in a huddle under the table on our boat, with all the blankets and our flea bags over me and rewound 42 feet of film by hand. I don't know what the trouble was but I suppose I did something stupid when I put the film in the camera the other day on the bear trail by the lake.

(August 31, 1940)

Albert Georgeson has arrived to work for Jim. I had a conversation with him about his relations on Galiano Id. etc. but had to write everything as he is quite deaf.

(August 2, 1941)

We went up with all the boats to the head of the inlet and anchored in the Thumming River near its mouth, opposite Barnes' place. We took Jack over to a point half way between the waterfall and Snout Point, where Dan and the boys were falling trees into the sea. I took movies of this. Afterwards, Dan and Ernie Flemming and Bert Barber came on board and we all had dinner. They had felled a big stick over a hundred feet long. After dinner we towed this log across the inlet, the boys helping with their dugout.

(August 9, 1941)

When hand-loggers' licences were first authorized in 1885 there were no restrictions on method and a logger could cut ungranted timber of the Crown in any locality whatsoever. In 1906 a provision was introduced which forbade the use of steam machinery. Some loggers risked the fine and hired donkey engines (so-called because they had less power than a horse) to drag the logs into the sea. The hand-logger worked with double-bitted axe, peavey and Gilchrist jack, using great skill and ingenuity to harness the force of gravity to slide the great logs splashing into the water. Logs have been known to run half a mile to the salt water, bouncing down the mountain slopes at high and dangerous speeds. It has been estimated that there were at least 4,000 hand-loggers on the coast, but the numbers declined steadily after 1915, when most of the easily accessible slopes rising sheer from the inlets had been logged off. Today, under new licensing, second-growth timber is being hand-logged in the Bella Coola area, still with hand tools only.

Amy went off in the morning and caught a snapper. We left our snug tie-up and Jim Stapleton left shortly after us in his boat. We were all bound for Slim's place in Ramsay Arm. We ran into Salmon Bay to look for a pictograph which we found at the

west entrance. It was an interesting one. I suppose an eagle
carrying off a salmon.

(August 13, 1938)

We went ashore and talked to Slim, who had given Stapleton
some nice Indian things for us. Amy and I found one or two ar-
rowheads on the beach, very different from ours at home
where there is clamshell. Slim and Jim came to dinner with us
and in the afternoon Amy and I went in *Toketie* to Rounds and
Burchartt camp close by to look for a picto which we found just
to the left of the freight shed, on a rocky bluff. After I had made
a sketch, I went up to the camp, and the watchman ran me
down to the end of the wharf on the gas speeder. Slim is a Nova
Scotian, a fine type of man, very independent. He would give
you anything and take nothing. He traps in the winter, and also
catches prawns. He sets his prawn traps at a depth of 600 feet.
He says there are fine prawns in all these deep inlets.

(August 14, 1938)

Leaving Ramsey Arm, Barrow steered the *Toketie* southwest, re-
entering Calm Channel, then north to Stuart Island, the hub of the
area.

Arrived at Stuart Id. In the afternoon we went to see Mr. Betts,
our old logger friend with the wooden leg. He is quite a philos-
opher, and if more people had the same outlook on life it
would be far better. He gets the old age pension of $20 a
month. He gave us a couple of eggs each for our breakfast.
Louis Le Blanc tied up by us later, aboard his troller *Thetis*. He
had run up here from Nanaimo in 16 hours. The *Thetis* is a
splendid type of boat, built by Volmers at Nanaimo, and Le
Blanc keeps her in first class shape. It is a pleasure to look at
her. Gerrard came on board for a yarn and a cup of coffee after
he had put about two tons of salmon on Hatashita's fish packer.

This is the same Matt Gerrard who later retired to Quadra Island,
where the Barrows met Mrs. Gerrard and Dorris in an earlier chapter of this book.

We left after lunch for Parrish's and tied up at his float. He
looked at my Auto Lite generator and pronounced that there is
a short circuit in it, no doubt causing it to be dumb. He is or-

dering a new insulation & new brushes which will be here in a
week. We looked at the Westinghouse generator and found
that I had the charging wire on the low terminal instead of the
high, so that trouble, I think, is O.K. After tea at the Parrish's
house we returned to the Landing.

(August 3, 1938)

Received a visit from Mr. Radford, art editor of the Vancouver
Sun, who we met last year. Gerrard came on board later, and
Mrs. Gerrard and Dick. We met Angus Ker and his brother,
who had also left Toba Inlet where the fishing was N.G. They
were going on to Loughborough Inlet to fish. I took a snapshot
of them as they wanted one to send to their sister in Scotland.

(July 27, 1940)

Got up at 5 A.M. and made the trip up to the head of Bute Inlet
on the Union Steamship Co's *Chelohsin*. She arrived at Stuart Id.
about 6.30 A.M. and we were very pleased to go down to breakfast at 7. The skipper, Capt. Muir, was very pleasant to us, and
we had a long yarn with him when we went on deck. We talked
a lot with a Vancouver man who had spent many years in Pata-
gonia. We called at logging camps on the way up and also coming down. Mr. Allison, who owns the camp at the head of Bute,
sat with us at lunch. Rinnie and Nanette pleased the passengers, and had a fine lunch of bones. Deer flies at the head of the
Inlet attacked most people viciously but I escaped. We got back
to Stuart Id about 3 P.M. after a very pleasant busman's holiday.

(July 16, 1934)

If there is a logo for the Inside Coast during the first half of the
twentieth century, it would surely be the black-topped red funnel
of the Union Steamships, and the leit-motif would be the sound of
their whistles. They were familiar family friends to the people who
used them – *Cutch, Capilano, Comox, Coquitlam, Camosun, Chilkoot,
Cassiar, Chelohsin, Chilcotin, Cardena, Catala* – each with her own
personality and idiosyncrasies. The glamorous *Cardena*, on the
company letterhead and the flagship for a time, was longest in service (1923–1959), with the *Venture* a close second (1911–1946). The
Cassiar with her big handwheel like an old sailing ship, went into
every camp as far as Queen Charlotte Sound. The loggers could
wear their caulked boots on the *Cassiar* but not on any other ship.

Altogether there were 51 ships in the Union Steamship fleet, at different times.

The company was established in 1889 by a small group of Vancouver businessmen. The first coastal steamer was the *Cutch,* pressed into service while three new steamers were being constructed: the *Capilano,* the *Comox* and the *Coquitlam.* The company survived the hard times of the First World War and had a second expansionist period during the 1920s, when the excursion business was developed; the Barrows watched the crowds disembarking at Savary Island. However, as early as 1926 the company's annual report sounded a warning:

> "Logging conditions continue uncertain and the company is by no means deriving the amount of revenue from this source as formerly. This is partly due to the fact that log production has been reduced and partly due to the changing conditions of the logging operations. The modern tendency is to mass production at specific points with the result that the scattered camps with the hand-logging system are being gradually eliminated."[1]

Already the life of the coast was beginning to ebb. Lester Peterson's article "British Columbia's Depopulated Coast" describes how increasing centralization of the logging industry was accompanied by the same trend in fishing. As steamship schedules were cut back, the number of homesteaders decreased, for they needed transportation for their vegetables, meats and dairy products. Some could not endure the loneliness. Many of the Indian people were moving to the cities, and the government encouraged isolated bands to join established settlements nearer urban centres, to simplify the provision of services. The thousands of cannery workers no longer moved into the area, a seasonal migration like the fish they once canned. New cargoes – pulp and wood chips – were efficiently moved by barges. Float-planes and new roads further eroded steamboat travel. By 1959 the remaining ships of the Union Steamship Company were sold, bringing to an end 70 years of service. Francis and Amy Barrow, standing on the scrubbed wood decks and leaning on the rail of the *Chelohsin,* and later going below for an excellent meal in the varnished lounge, did not realize that in another 25 years, the steamship service would be a thing of the past.

When the complexity of tide-ripped passages and the lack of navigation aids is considered, the safety record of the company is remarkable. One master drew the outlines of the mountains in his log-book, to help him steer the course. Exact log-books were kept, each course run for a specific length of time at a precise speed, then the direction altered. However, in fog, most of the captains depended on navigation by whistle, giving a short blast and timing the return of the echo. If the sound returned in three seconds, the land was a quarter-mile off. Unfortunately the submerged "propeller-inspectors" reflected no echo. The steamships were quiet, so that a sharp, clear echo could be heard; the noisier diesels made the system less efficient. There was the additional hazard of navigation at night, when the moon would throw the black shadow of a mountain across the route, and the problem of fishboats at night, with a lantern at the end of the net but no way of knowing which lantern belonged to which vessel. In Peter Chapman's book *Navigating the Coast,* Captain Naughty is quoted as saying,

> "a lantern here and a lantern there and there'd be millions of them and you wonder, holy mackerel, how am I going to get through here, and you blow your whistle, four long blasts: I'M COMING! You can't stop. Tide's going to get you."[2]

Still at Stuart Island, Barrow recorded some of the interesting visitors they met there.

> The *Chelohsin* came in with mail and freight about 5 A.M. and there was a lot of moving of boats. We went down to the Hetzler's float at 11:30 A.M. and walked over the trail from there to the Anderson's who live at Whirlpool Lodge. Soon the tide started to race by, and when it was running strong the swirls and overfalls were a sight! Fellows were fishing from small boats in the back eddy just out of the racing tide, and caught a good many salmon. It was a sight worth seeing. Capt. Kiphart came and had a yarn. He later got an Indian to take him out into the back eddy and he took some shots of the rapids with a small movie camera. He left Tacoma in a 12-foot rowing boat with a small sail and intended rowing to Alaska. However, at Cape Caution, Queen Charlotte Sound, he had to give up owing to weather, and returned south. When he gets back to Tacoma he will have travelled 1000 miles in his small boat. He is

taking educational films. He walked back with us to the Hetzler's and had tea with us and told us a lot about his trip, very interesting and amusing in spots, and far from amusing in others.
He broadcasted in Seattle before he left and I read in the papers
about his intended trip and I felt sure we would meet him
somewhere. Mrs. Hetzler came on board with her daughter
and brought us a nice bunch of flowers from her very pretty
garden. The Barrymores of film fame are anchored further up
the rapids and Mr. Radford is anxious that we should meet
them, but we are no more anxious to meet film stars than they
would be to meet pictographic racketeers. The famous Dolores
[Barrymore] has been to the wharf here several times today and
she had the pleasure of seeing Matt Gerrard cutting my hair in
the wharf shed. In the evening we went to Parish's, to get him
to take up on the reverse gear and I had to leave the Johnson
overboard motor with him as the Powell River robbers had
made a rotten job of replacing the new coil. Fish boats come in
every day on their way south from Rivers Inlet. The salmon run
there has been a failure this year and the poor fellows are returning with very little money. They are fine chaps. The *Anna E.*
came in this evening, people going to see their son at the logging camp at Port Neville. They had two cocker spaniel pups
on board and Rinnie and Nannie were most interested in them.

(July 20, 1934)

I forgot to mention that on Sunday when we were at Whirlpool
Lodge, Mr. Anderson gave us some excellent smoked salmon
which he had just taken out of his smoke-house. Ran to Mr.
Parrish's for the Johnson which he had made a good job of. In
the afternoon the *Outcall* from Tacoma arrived with between 30
and 40 Sea Scouts on board. They were on their way back from
Alert Bay. They were a well-behaved bunch of boys and looked
after by a very pleasant lot of officers. The *Lady Evelyn* arrived
about 4 A.M. with mail and freight.

(July 31, 1934)

Separating the northern tip of Stuart Island from the mainland is
a narrow pass called the Arran Rapids where the tide can run nine
knots strong. Here lived the Sticklands.

Ran to Mr. George Stickland's where we made fast to the
boom. He came down to greet us. Mr. Stickland said he would

be pleased to come over with us to the Arran Rapids where I wanted to take a movie. He said 2.30 was the time to go over, but after dinner rain started and it continued all through the night, putting a stop to our expedition. Mr. and Mrs. Stickland came on board to tea and supper and we had two sessions of three-handed crib. Mr. Stickland gave us some nice Indian things for our collection. He said, when we arrived in the morning, we had travelled down the rapids two and a half hours before slack water. I noticed some swirls and cross currents by the Gillard Ids. but they did not worry *Toketie* in the least. It was not the big tide of the day and I understood from Jack that it was O.K. to go to Stickland's any time on a small tide. Stickland said it is better when going to his place, which is situated on the west side of Vancouver Bay, from the S.E. end of the Rapids. But on a flood tide when going to the other end of the Rapids, keep to the east of the Gillard Islands.

(August 16, 1938)

Stickland and I took the row boat to the point close to the west entrance of the Arran Rapids and went ashore and I took several movies. It was only a half tide, but there was a great disturbance of water. It must be a wonderful sight on a zero tide. I believe there is a drop of eight feet in the middle.

(August 17, 1938)

Concerning the Arran Rapids, the *Sailing Directions, British Columbia Coast* advises: "The channel is little used and should only be attempted at or near slack water."[3] Leaving the mecca of Stuart Island, the *Toketie* motored northwest into Cordero Channel, but stopped almost immediately near Dent Island, where Barrow marvelled at a new piece of machinery, part of the process of change.

We left for Percy Belson's camp, just beyond Dent Island. Mac greeted us and helped us to make fast to Percy's float. We went ashore and I took some movies of Percy bulldozing trees, stumps, etc. with the cat, to make a road for hauling out logs. It is a wonderful machine and it is certainly surprising what a lot of road Percy has cleared in a week. After dinner I took a movie of Percy's house and the camp.

(August 18, 1938)

An "arm" in nautical language is a short inlet. Northwest up Cordero Channel from Belson's camp is Frederick Arm, poking into the mainland mountain rib.

> Ran to Frederick Arm and anchored off Mr. Chapman's house. He was in his row boat and came on board. We asked him if he would pilot us into the Estero Basin and he said he would be pleased to do so. We are going there tomorrow and Mr. Chapman is going to bring some traps along and set them for cougar. We went ashore and saw his splendid garden. He brought out his furs and showed us bear, cougar, wolf, martin and mink. Some of the cougar and wolf pelts are very big. One cougar he shot was just about six feet from his house.
>
> (August 8, 1934)

> I worked on the Johnson motor as the water circulating pipes were stopped up. This I remedied, but the engine still only runs on one cylinder, and as far as I can see I wasted my money at Powell River and Stuart Id. on mechanics. We were going to run the row-boat into the Estero Basin today with the Johnson motor, as there is only one tide a day to get in. However, as the Johnson was not running properly this was not possible and the plan is to go in tomorrow at high tide with the *Toketie* and stay in over night.
>
> (August 8, 1934)

> Left Mr. Chapman's at 12.30 for the narrows at the mouth of the Estero Basin and tied up to the boom there as the tide was running out very fast. We were going to have lunch there, but Mr. Duncan who lives at the mouth called over to us to say that they were going to float a lot of boomsticks through the narrows and as we might have got pinched where we were lying, and as the tide had slacked up a bit, we decided to go through. We bumped quite a few rocks and bent all the blades of the propeller, but I don't think much harm has been done. We should have waited for another hour, or possibly two or three. We tied to an overhanging tree by a fine little creek and had lunch. There is hardly any tide inside the Estero Basin. A bear trail led along the beach. We then went to the head of the Estero Basin and Chapman and I went along an old log road and

Chapman set a trap for cougar in an animal trail. We then went back and anchored for the night in a sheltered bay. We went ashore and picked a billy full of huckleberries and salal berries. The bears had been busy before us and had stripped a lot of the fruit. We caught a nice lot of tommy-cod close to the *Toketie* and had a fine supper of vegetables, a salad from Chapman's garden, and meat. Stewed huckleberries and one-minute tapioca pudding finished off the meal. Afterwards Chapman and I went over in the row boat, the Johnson motor propelling us on one cylinder, to Judd Moore's logging camp across the Basin. Chapman saw a friend and I saw Ruggs, whom we used to see at the Yaculta Rapids. It was an awful dismal camp and everyone looked dejected.

(August 9, 1934)

Had a fine breakfast of stewed fruit and fried tommy-cod and bacon. Chapman slept under the trees at the point on a bed of deep moss with his dog. After breakfast I took photos and sketched a group of old pictographs close to our anchorage. We moved up towards the mouth of the Basin, where there is a logging camp, and tied up to the boom. There was about the steepest log chute we had ever seen. After lunch we moved up to the narrows and tied up to a float. Here we met Mr. Duncan doing some blacksmith work. We watched the narrows till the tide had finished running into the Basin and then we went slowly through and did not bump any rocks. I would not care to go in again except on a 23-foot Prince Rupert tide, and one would always have to be careful. The stream flows out of Estero Basin till high tide outside and the time of slack water in the narrows seems to be governed entirely by the amount of water in the Basin. The boom man had just shut the entrance to the boom just outside the narrows as they were just going to run a boom of logs through the narrows when we went through. We had an awful job opening the boom to get out, as the wind was blowing against the boom and we had to anchor *Toketie* and put a rope on the closing log and haul it across the opening. I do not think logging outfits have any legal right whatever to close the entrances to navigable waters, and we were foolish to bother about closing the infernal boom. At all events we lost today's catch of tommy-cod when the rowboat filled with water.

(August 10, 1934)

About 11 A.M. we left for Gomer Id., taking Chapman and his rowboat. On the east side of the island, on the mainland, I took photos and sketched a group of pictographs while Amy and Chapman rowed round and fished. After lunch we said good-bye to our trapper friend [Chapman].

(August 11, 1934)

Travelling southeast down Nodales Channel, the *Toketie* entered the wide opening to both Thurston Bay and Cameleon Harbour on Sonora Island.

Dropped the hook in Handfield Bay. In the morning we went ashore and met some people named Wallbanks. They had a nice sunny spot facing south and their garden was deep mid-den. Wallbanks went off to Thurston Bay as the *Chelohsin* was expected, and his wife came to lunch with us. We looked around on the beaches where there was wonderful midden and Amy found a pecked anchor stone. Later on we went further up the harbour to Mr. Edric Lansall's place but they were all away getting mail. They have a very pleasant place and a nice garden. They returned soon after our arrival and Mrs. Lansall and her daughter came on board. Mr. Lansall suffers much, one of his legs being damaged, and arthritis worrying him all the time. They have found a good many Indian stone implements on their place and the house site evidently ran all along where their orchard is now. They sent their finds to the Provincial Museum. There is no doubt that in days gone by this harbour was used by very many Indians. Macamoose said that when he was a boy he saw this place crowded with canoes.

(August 18, 1936)

We went ashore and visited Mr. Sondey, a Czechoslovakian, whose home was close to where we were anchored. He had been a toolmaker in his country, and in Italy. He was a funny little man clothed in underwear and a carpenter's apron. He has to do a lot of work to produce vegetables as the ground is rock and it seems to lack humus. He gave us an arrow point he found in his garden.

(August 29, 1938)

We ran to Thurston Bay and I had a yarn with Mr. Boon of the *Persepa* and shortly after we moved to the landlocked harbour at the south side of the bay, about a mile from the Forestry Station. This bay is not marked on the chart and Thurston Bay has only been roughly charted. Shortly before dark Tom arrived, the *B.C. Forester* having returned. We had a talk and Tom returned to the Station about 11. He found it rather puzzling to find the exit of this landlocked harbour in the dark, as he had never been in before. The searchlight however gave him a lead.

(August 27, 1938)

The government forestry station at Thurston Bay was established in 1914, to serve as fuel storage and repair depot for the fleet of the B.C. Forest Branch, which had been established in 1912 under the Department of Lands. In 1945 the name was changed to the Forest Service of the Department of Lands and Forests. The title is still commonly used as a variant name of the present Ministry of Forests. Today only a rusting Pelton wheel, which once supplied electricity, survives to mark the site of the floats, ways, boat storage and construction sheds, houses and bunkhouses of the Thurston Bay Forestry Station, where the 57-foot flagship, the *B.C. Forester,* was built in 1923. Although the little settlement included rangers, engineers, ship builders and their families, there was no school or hospital and few people wished to live in this lonely place. In the late Thirties the depot was considered to be too far from sources of supplies, and was moved to a site on the Fraser River. In 1941 everything of value was removed from the Thurston Bay site and most of the buildings were burned.

In 1927, besides the large station at Thurston Bay, the Vancouver Forest District had 15 boat stations on the Inside Coast, some consisting of only a small house and storage shed on a rock bluff, with dock below. As so many of the logging operations involved less than a half-dozen men, a ranger might be dealing with 50 to 60 operations in his territory.

In the morning we went over to the Forestry Station and made fast to the float. Tom showed me over his ship and we met some more of his friends.

(August 28, 1938)

Retracing their route, the Barrows headed north up Nodales

Channel, then turned westward into Cordero Channel, to reach the store at Thurlow Bay, on West Thurlow Island.

Bucked the tide all the way to Shoal Bay. Here we were greeted by old Nye who once lived in Regency Square, Brighton, the storekeeper's handyman. Amy cooked roast lamb, carrots and potatoes, and a trifle: some feed. We got bread, the *Chelohsin* having arrived just before us with freight and mail.

(August 1, 1934)

We met the local Fishery Warden at the wharf, Mr. Gregson. He asked me if I had ever met an old man and his wife who cruised up the coast taking photographs of Indian paintings. I had to tell him that I was that old man. We got gas and groceries at Thompson's store. After supper we met another Thompson who lives here. His wife has been away in Vancouver for some time, getting treatment for goitre. There is another fire near Rock Bay so smoke which has appeared will not help photography.

(August 25, 1938)

Perhaps Joe Gregson could be designated the archetypal pioneer, the unsung hero. He died in the Sechelt hospital at the age of 95 and his friend Bill Law spoke of "his honesty and unfailing consideration of others". When he retired from his work as warden in the Granite Bay and Philipps Arm region, he wrote a brief account of his life, ending with the statement: "I am glad that I had a hand in making Canada what it is today."[4]

Born in Blackpool, one of a family of 15, Joe ran away from an apprenticeship to a blacksmith and at the age of 14 shipped out on a North Sea trawler. For four dollars a month he had to haul the net in by hand every six hours, clean and stow the fish and then snatch a bit of food before the next haul. "In the winter it was so cold that I would sometimes cry from the pain." After serving in the Boer War (where he became welterweight champion of the British Army) he came to British Columbia and cleared lots on Granville Street for $25 per lot; as it took about a month to clear one lot, Joe figured he made five cents an hour. Next, he made bricks for the first Vancouver General Hospital. Later, he went to the logging camps where he "knew pretty near all the loggers on the coast". He then established his own brickyard in Storm Bay, Sechelt Inlet, and at the same time did hand-logging. Returning in his old age to fishing, he was soon made a warden, the work in hand when Barrow met him. In his review of his own life, he ends with the comment that "conditions are far better for the working class than they were when I first came here", demonstrating that consideration for others which Bill Law remembered.[5]

I had a yarn with a cast iron junk collector who was waiting with his boat to catch the slack through the Yaculta Rapids. He seemed to know all the nooks and crannies up the coast as well as we do. Gill netters from Rivers Inlet are returning south and they have had a very poor season.

(August 1, 1939)

Across Cordero Channel from Shoal Bay, stubby Philipps Arm, only about five miles long, thrusts into the mainland.

Going up Philipps Arm we passed the Julie, Alexandra and Hercules mines. They looked in rather a sickly state and I don't suppose they do much more than sell stock to suckers. We tied up for the night to Mr. Macleod's float and he came to supper.

(August 6, 1934)

We rowed after breakfast about a mile to the river mouth where we hoped to find Johnny Macamoose at home, but nobody was at the house. We wanted to get some dried cakes of berries and oolichan oil. Macleod is going to get some from him for us, to pick up on our way down the coast. Macamoose has spent 16 years in jail and is a bit of a bad actor. A trader a good many years ago took up beads, calico, trinkets etc. to the north end of Vancouver Island to trade with the Indians. He vanished and was not seen again. Some time after, an Indian woman with whom Macamoose was living was found with some of the calico. On being asked where she got it, she said from Macamoose. The authorities were pretty certain Macamoose did the trader in, but they could not prove it, so they gave him a term in the coop. Macleod took us to some burial caves a short way along the shore from his house and we found one complete coffin box and some skulls and bones, but the best of the skulls had been taken by Vancouver dentists. A lot of big salmon and trout are caught up the river and Macleod amused us with tales of when he has taken the great and near-great up there, the Barrymores, Mr. Fleichman of yeast fame, Mr. Eastman of Kodak fame, etc. It is a really fine day.

(August 7, 1934)

Amy trolled for salmon but caught none, though they are jumping everywhere. In the words of old Chief Edward: "There are plenty of salmon but they are scarce." We rowed across Philipps Arm to see an old Indian dwelling site at the top of a bluff, very overgrown. In the afternoon Amy went trolling while Macleod and I went about ¾ of a mile down the Arm in Macleod's gas boat and jacked a fir log into the sea. Macleod wanted it for fire wood. He came to supper with us, which Amy had ready on our return. Macleod gave us a bag of potatoes and bottle of salmon which he had put up. We had it for supper and i t was fine.

(September 4, 1934)

Johnny Macamoose and Jess paddled alongside in the canoe for a chat. The Boeings are in a bay close by, the *Taconite*, their seaplane, speed boat and numerous other boats all there. I went ashore after breakfast and saw the boat Macleod is building, a 32-footer, but he has not got very far with her. He has a small saw-mill for cutting his planks and lumber. In the afternoon we johnsoned up to Johnny Macamoose and after a haggle bought Jenny's berry basket for $1.25. We then took a photo of the old couple in their canoe.

(July 18, 1935)

In the late afternoon I went ashore and helped Macleod sack up some charcoal which he had made, to use in his forge. Just at dusk Mr. Fleishman arrived in his palatial yacht *Haida*, and they anchored close by. At present the only boats here are the *Haida*, one of the biggest on the coast, and *Toketie*, one of the smallest. Macleod came back and we had a yarn with him, but he has me beaten at talking.

(August 26, 1938)

Leaving Philipps Arm and the talkative Mr. Macleod, the *Toketie* chugged west along Cordero Channel.

Went on to Crawford Anchorage [East Thurlow Island] and tied up to a Norwegian fisherman's float. After supper, rowed across to Erasmus Id. and visited Mr. Prichard, who struck Victoria and this coast in the 1880's. He used to come up the coast in a sloop and trade with the Indians and he told us of the wonderful things that could be bought for a song then. Visited Mrs. Johnson, from Sweden, at her house on the float we were tied up at. She seemed pleased to see us and asked us to call in again when we came south. She said she had been in the service of an English lady in Chicago. What a change to this place, where she sees very few people, and her husband is away all day, hand logging. We gave her a Bible study book, "Film Fun" and a "Daily Sketch". We then went over to Mr. Prichard and tied up at his float. He came aboard and talked about the Economic Conference, Archaeology, old days in Victoria, and the time to get through the Greene Point Rapids and Whirlpool Rapids, Wellbore Channel.

(July 18, 1933)

A tug passed, towing a logging outfit, eight houses, A-frame and donkey. We rowed over to a small island close to where we were anchored and found four or five burial houses on it. They had fallen down and a good many skulls and bones were scattered about, and a good many in the coffin boxes. I selected a skull which had most of its teeth, for our dentist. At 3.20 P.M. we continued through Greene Point Rapids, bucking the tide. I took a photo of the pictograph opposite Erasmus Id.

(September 3, 1934)

I lost the chance of an interesting movie when walking along the beach, by not having my camera with me. A snake had just caught a sand eel about five inches long, which it held by the head. The eel was thrashing about, trying to free itself, but by the time I returned with the camera the snake had swallowed the eel and lay basking in the sun.

(August 2, 1939)

Westward once more along Cordero Channel, the Barrows set off to explore Loughborough Inlet, stopping first at Beaver Creek, a small, narrow bay providing safe anchorage. Beaver Creek is sometimes called Beaver Inlet.

While I was frying eggs and bacon Mr. Fox came along the boom to pump out his boat. He invited us to the house on a little bay close by. After breakfast we rowed round and met Mr. Fox's mother and wife. They have a nice house on logs, but it is not floating. All the ground nearby is kitchen midden and their vegetable garden is splendid. They gave us some turnips and would have given us other vegetables only we still have a supply. The Foxes insisted on us staying to dinner and later on they came out to *Toketie*. We bought some eggs from them and Mrs. Fox gave Amy some magnificent dahlias. Fox is not running his camp at present and I fear has suffered from times of depression. He has a railway track up the valley for some distance. The present prices for logs are not encouraging.

(August 2, 1934)

Shortly after breakfast we received a visit from the Fox family and their three dogs, which walk along the boom sticks like old time loggers. They gave us some green peas and a can of something they had put up, but as they did not say what it was we do not know if it is meat or fruit, but we will find out some day.

(August 3, 1934)

The following year, when the Barrows came to visit the Fox family they found Colonel Rawlstone of Cowichan Bay in charge of the Fox lumber camp. He was planning to bring the logs out by truck instead of using the railway.

After lunch we moved to the mouth of Beaver Creek and tied up at Mr. Green's float. We noticed his well-kept little farm, situated on an old Indian house site. Mr. and Mrs. Green received us in a kindly manner and after a chat we gave the dogs a run in their meadow. In the evening we visited the Greens again and they gave us a bottle of milk, a lovely bunch of flowers and a big bundle of magazines. Mr. Green had been carrying hay today and was tired, so we left early.

(July 22, 1935)

In the morning I helped Green get in the last few cocks of hay and the Greens came to lunch with us. Whilst preparing for them, Amy ran a sliver into her finger from one of the cedar locker lids, the coffee spilt all over the shelf and boat, the lid coming off the tin, and while I was cleaning up, the milk upset in the bread tin. The Greens have three nice Jersey cows and a bull, and it is well to keep inside the fence when visiting their place. At 9 P.M. the Union boat called at Roy, just across the inlet and people went straight over for their mail as they don't like to leave it there, since the Postmaster has the reputation for going through it.

(July 23, 1935)

After saying good-bye we left for Grey Creek across Loughborough Inlet. We soon found the petroglyph and Mr. Myers, the only man living at this spot, came over from his shack and had a yarn. I took photos of it but several times was interrupted by the rain, showers coming down at intervals all day. This was a place of 150 people a few years ago when the shingle mill was running, but now it is inhabited by one old man. The houses are all tumbled down, and the school house is the only building that looks inhabitable. In the afternoon we rowed over to the smaller of the two islands in front of the creek and looked at the burial caves there. There were a number of skulls and bones lying around but Mr. Myers said the kids used to go over from the village and hunt for heads etc. in the caves, and everything of that kind has been looted. Myers came to tea with us, and we anchored for the night close to the small island. It is a good sheltered spot.

(August 2, 1934)

It has rained steadily for the past 24 hours and I expect there is a south-easter blowing down Johnstone Strait. However, this is a fine sheltered spot worth knowing. We spent the day reading, letter writing, and Amy made a sketch of me while I was making coloured sketches of pictographs. Towards evening I baled the rainwater out of the rowboat, and we went ashore at the mouth of the creek, got some water and gave the dogs a run. Myers says one can see wolf, cougar and bear tracks a short way up the creek, and the deer are about cleaned out. In the next bay north a good many years ago was the village of Roy, with quite a number of people living there. The news of the Klondyke rush came and they all left their mining industry here, leaving also furniture, houses and everything, beating it for the north. The present Roy is about two miles north of here. Just a few people living there, and the postmaster who is famous for opening everyone's mail and learning about their private matters. People have complained to the Post Office Department, but nothing happens, and the postmaster at Roy just laughs and goes on opening people's mail. The glass is going down so I expect we shall have some more rain.

(August 4, 1934)

Plenty of rain coming down so we decided to remain in this good anchorage. About noon a fishing boat came and anchored by us and I went over and had a yarn. Two very pleasant young fellows from Redonda Id. They were on their way back from Rivers Inlet. They said all sorts and kinds of boats were there, and most had not a chance of getting fish. The sea lions were very bad in the nets, doing much damage. They said about 8 fellows were drowned and one done in. They told me an amusing story about the "Roaring Hole" up at Mackenzie Sound. They told the fishery Warden that there were often salmon in the big salt lagoon through the "Roaring Hole". He said "I have never been in there. I will go and see!" He went off & did not appear again for 4 or 5 days. When he met them he put on a sickly smile and said he had knocked his rudder off in the narrows and had had quite a time of it. He was quite impressed with the terrific strength of the tide at the "Roaring Hole". My friends said they could have poached all the rivers in the district while he was away. I rowed Amy round the island. She got a blueback salmon in a very short time on a No. 5 Wonder spoon. We shared the salmon with the old man ashore and had some for supper and it was very good.

(August 5, 1934)

Ran to Heydon Bay, north up Loughborough, and made fast to the Heydon Bay Gold Mine float. The place is deserted and no sign of the floating store. A fishery warden came in soon after our arrival. He said the store had moved down to Pender Harbour. Sockeyes are splashing about all over the bay. Mr. Baker arrived from Roy and put his gill net on the rack to mend as a blackfish had gone through it. By one of the mine buildings I noted a case of empty Enos Fruit Salt bottles; there must have been over 100 of them, and I thought that perhaps the water at the camp might be mineralized and Enos was necessary to counteract its bad effects. Mr. Baker was able, however, to ex-

plain the mountain of empty bottles. He said that some of the
people at the mine were fond of rum and that the Enos was
used in the sobering up process.

(July 25, 1935)

Returning southwards down Loughborough Inlet, the *Toketie*
paused at Beaver Creek so that the Barrows could buy some fresh
home-made bread from Mrs. Green. Leaving Loughborough, they
entered Cordero Channel at the point where it becomes Chancellor Channel. Proceeding westward along Chancellor Channel
for a few miles, they turned northward up Wellbore Channel and
then made an abrupt turn to starboard into the sheltered anchorage in Forward Harbour.

Heavy rain as we got near Forward Harbour. However, it has
cleared away, 11 A.M. There is a good deal of smoke about, due
to forest fires further down the coast. Johnsoned out of Forward Harbour and into Bessborough Bay to the north and went
ashore at Mr. McCulloch's place. He is a trapper. He did not
know of any pictographs in Forward Harbour but said the Pembridges in the next little bay might know. They did not, but we
got some eggs from them. McCulloch came on board about
7 P.M. after we had looked at his garden close by our anchorage.
The Pembridges had their cat and some poultry recently carried off by cougar. McCulloch said he saw a large bear a few
days ago at the flat by the river at the head of this harbour. I expect they will be on any of these grass flats at the river mouths,
especially when the salmon start going up.

(August 28, 1933)

Returning to Forward Harbour, we anchored at the head of the
harbour. On landing near the old house site near Worly Stream
we very soon found the flat boulder covered with petroglyphs
which Mac and Percy had told us about. It is a very fine example of the incised art, and is comparable to the petroglyphs
at Nanaimo, though there are not as many figures. It is on granite and looks very old. After lunch we rowed to another old
house site at the opposite side of the harbour. We examined a
cut in the midden about ten feet deep, where logs had been
hauled out. It looked like an archaeologist's paradise but we
found nothing. The wind died down at dusk, for which God be

praised. We are the sole occupants of this harbour.

(August 21, 1938)

Amy found another boulder on which were other petroglyphs. Percy had said something about it when we were at his camp. The pecking was not so deep as in the other group, possibly owing to sea action, though both petroglyph boulders are under water at high tide.

(August 22, 1938)

Ran to Jackson Bay in Topaze Harbour, where I made fast to a float where I thought the store was. A young fellow named Fearing came down to the boat, and he informed us that there had not been a store in Jackson Bay for some years. Amy went up to the house to buy some fresh milk and eggs from his mother, and I had a shave. Mrs. Fearing insisted on us coming to dinner with them. Just before we sat down, her husband and other son came in, having returned from towing a float house from Port Neville to a spot near Shawn Pt. in Sunderland Channel. It certainly is a beautiful summer day. A great treat after the windy days we have had lately. The Fearings have a nice place, a lot of it midden. They have found a few things which they showed us. Fearing has a lot of bees and we bought a tin of the clearest honey I have ever seen, from clover and fire-weed. The son who arrived with his father played to us on his piano-accordion. The house seemed full of musical instruments of one sort or another.

(August 22, 1938)

In the afternoon we all piled into *Toketie* and ran over to Eng's camp in Read Bay at the head of Topaze Harbour. They have bulldozed the two big mounds of midden, the one on the left being nearly cleared away. They have cut the face of the other to make a space to house the cat diesel tractors, and the wall of clam shell and earth must be at least 30 feet high, a wonderful Indian house site indeed. The part of the midden that has been cleared away has been used to make a fill in front of the tractor shed. I took some movies of this colossal shell heap. Mrs. Eng showed us some Indian stuff that had been found, including a very fine diorite horizontal hammer with a face deeply carved on it. She showed us also some carved wooden panels she had from a grave site near Roy in Loughborough Inlet. They represented faces. She said she had taken off the abalone inlay on them, also the hair that was attached all round the carving, there being small holes round the outer edge to secure the hair in. She said she did not like the hair. Too bad.

(September 5, 1939)

Belatedly, British Columbians have recognized the cultural value of the Indian middens, the garbage accumulation from thousands of years, in which the record of our coastal prehistory is hidden. Since 1960, midden and burial sites and rock-art sites have been protected by the British Columbia Archaeological and Historical Sites Protection Act, which prescribes a penalty of $1,000 fine and six months in jail for anyone who should "destroy, desecrate, deface, move, excavate, or alter in any way a designated site or remove from it an object, or destroy, desecrate or alter a burial-place or remove from it skeletal remains, or destroy, deface, alter, excavate or dig in an Indian kitchen-midden, shell-heap, house-pit, cave or other habitation site, or a cairn, mound, fortification or other site or object, situated on Crown lands."[6] The Act came too late to save many important archaeological sites.

We got some milk, butter and canned fruit from the Fearings and about 9 o'clock they came along in their boat and we in ours to Aquilar Point at the head of Sunderland Channel, and we landed where one of the boys had been told about a cave. We found an old-time coffin box, only the sides remaining, tooled with straight grooves. The place had been raided and there were not even bones about.

(September 6, 1939)

Ran to Sunderland Channel and I took a large photo of the pictograph Amy found. She went off fishing while I was busy with the camera, and returned to say she had found two more pictographs a little further on. I could get ashore at each spot and set up the tripod, and old *Toketie* never moved, tied up to a piece of kelp. The day was very fine and not a ripple on the water.

(August 16, 1936)

Leaving Topaze Harbour, the Barrows headed west, out Sunderland Channel into Johnstone Strait, early in the morning. An early

Guide to Mariners warns: "We advise all good sailors to travel Johnstone Strait between dawn and noon, and not linger".[7]
Well before noon, they had turned into the narrow opening of
sheltered Port Neville.

> We are now tied up to the float by Hansen's store. Got some
> cow's milk.
>
> (July 19, 1933)

Of all the coastal pioneers named Hansen, probably none are better known than the Hansens of Port Neville. Karen Hansen, who
sold milk to the Barrows in 1933, ran the post office from 1920 to
1956, living in the huge log house/store/post office which her father
had built and which still stands. Her father, Hans Hansen, born in
Tonsberg, Norway, came to this distant inlet in 1891, having left
home at the age of 14 as a cabin boy on the sailing ship *Esmeralda*.
He jumped ship at Vancouver in 1877 and took a job at the Hastings
Mill, intending to return to Norway with his earnings. But one day
when he was duck hunting in False Creek, his old muzzle-loader
exploded, shattering his hand. The local blacksmith made an iron
rig for his arm, with a square hole into which an oar fitted. Soon he
bought a sloop, loaded it with goods, and set off up the coast to
trade with the Indians. Arriving at Port Neville, he recognized the
place of his dreams. He built a small house, married and had a son,
Billy. When his wife died, leaving him with a four-year-old, Hansen
journeyed to Norway where he was fortunate to find Kathinka
Marie, who has left an account of her life in Frances Duncan's book
The Sayward-Kelsey Bay Saga. Kathinka Marie learned English from
Billy and he learned Norwegian from her.

A photograph of Kathinka's family taken about 1924 shows them
aboard their boat, with Karen on the float, brother Arthur strad-
dling the bow, sisters Lilly and Edith on the roof, and brother Olaf
and father Hans in the stern. By this time the huge log house had
been built, 32 by 48 feet, two storeys high, with porches across front
and back. The great logs had to be hoisted into place with hand
winch, block and tackle. The orchard was doing well and cows had
been bought from the Halliday farm at Kingcome Inlet. From an
extensive garden the Hansens were shipping produce to Port
Harvey. By the time of the family photograph, Hans Hansen was
becoming blind, but the family took over management of the place

and Hans lived happily in the log house until his death in 1939, six years after that day the Barrows called in to buy milk.

Hans Hansen's daughter, Edith, in 1975 wrote a tribute to the Columbia Coast Mission ship *Columbia* and to the mission's founder, John Antle. Her mother, Kathinka Marie, had only been at Port Neville a year when John Antle and his young son arrived, cold and wet, on that first expedition in their 14-foot sailboat *Laverock*. She remembered a timid knock at the door, and a shivering boy looking up at her. The visit established a lifelong friendship. Mrs. Hansen was unwell much of her life, and often one of the Hansen children had to go to Kelsey Bay to telegraph for the *Columbia* to come, and come they did, sometimes through terrible seas in Johnstone Strait. "The doctors we knew best in the late 1920s and 1930s were Kirkpatrick, Ryan and F. Herschel Stringer." The *Columbia* also brought books and films and Christmas parties, with Cecil Fitzgerald, the engineer, making a very jolly Santa. Then the Hansen children grew up and Edith tells how the *Columbia* steamed upcoast first for her brother's wedding, then for her sister's, and then "in June of 1940, the *Columbia* came to Port Neville, this time bedecked with flags flying merrily in the breeze, and bringing Canon Greene to officiate at the marriage of my husband and myself. For this afternoon wedding, more than 100 people arrived by boat from far and near, mostly flying flags and laden with guests to cram into the little chapel aboard, to hear our wedding vows."[8]

During these years the fishing industry changed. Hans Hansen said that when the main fishing in Johnstone Strait was trolling, there was good business in the Port Neville store. Then the seine boats and gillnetters took over and the trollers tended to go farther north or around Cape Mudge to the south. Later, there were so many boats that there would only be three or four days of fishing weekly. The fishermen would fly in for those few days, leaving their cars at Kelsey Bay and their families in southern towns. Port Neville's store and post office were no longer needed.

We then moved up the harbour to Robbers' Nob, an interesting ancient Indian stronghold. This place, with sheer cliffs on three sides and a curious terraced approach on the fourth, was covered with midden. I took photographs of the petroglyphs on a flat granite outcropping of rock on the beach below. Later we walked along the beach and picked up a broken hammer and a nice point. We then moved a little further up the harbour and called on a Mrs. Allen & her son. They came on board *Toketie* and had tea with us. We went ashore after & saw their place and got some homemade bread and carrots from them. Mrs. Allen's husband was drowned in this harbour a year or two ago. The son looks ill and they want to leave here. It is a lonely place.

(July 19, 1933)

The Christenson family and ourselves, Salt Lagoon, Redonda Island, 1938.

Me, Amy, Bill Horth, Frank Shepheard, Frank Norris, Percy Belson, 1934.

The Gerrard family and ourselves, Stuart Island, 1935.

Mr. and Mrs. Dusenbury, Bodega Anchorage, 1939.

Jim Stapleton, Little Toba River, 1939.

The Champions, Mrs. Champion's sister and ourselves at their floating cabin, mouth of Toba Inlet, 1936.

Angus Kerr hauling in his gillnet, 1940.

The George Sticklands and ourselves, Arran Rapids, 1938.

Percy Belson's camp, Dent Island, 1938.

Mrs. Hatch and her little daughter, with Amy, Frederick Arm, 1939.

Tom Hunter at the Forestry Station, Thurston Bay, 1938.

Mr. Green with the last load of hay, Loughborough Inlet, 1935.

The Fearings and ourselves, Jackson Bay, Topaze Harbour, 1938.

Laurette and Jim Stanton, Knight Inlet, 1935.

Burial mound, Lulaladsi (Klaoitsis), 1934.

Mrs. Williams and Mrs. Wilson at Karlukwees village, 1934.

Karlukwees village, 1935.

The Pedersens and ourselves on their float in Beware Passage, Harbledown Island, 1936.

The Reynolds, Claydon Bay, 1939.

Doug and Bessie Dane, Ballenas Island lighthouse, 1935.

CHAPTER SIX

The islands and passages at the eastern end of Queen Charlotte Sound comprise the last and most northerly area of the Barrow travels. North of Port Neville, the next escape from the winds of the long, straight, water highway called Johnstone Strait is a turn to the east at Havannah Channel, into the sheltered waters of Port Harvey, on Cracroft Island.

Tied up at the Bennett's float. They no longer keep a store. They came down to *Toketie* and also a log scaler Mr. Fowler, who had been scaling their logs. We went up to the Bennett's and stayed there till midnight. On our way up the harbour we called at Mrs. Dawson's and got some eggs and bread.

(August 24, 1933)

Took Mr. and Mrs. Bennett and Martin Peterson to Forward Bay [southern shore of Cracroft Island, off Johnstone Strait] and visited Mrs. Forrest and Mrs. Powell there. We had lunch on *Toketie* in the bay. Mrs. Forrest and Mrs. Powell were coming back with us to stay at the Bennett's, but Mrs. Forrest was taken quite ill, and after she had been put to bed and Amy and Mrs. Powell had done all they could for her, we returned to Port Harvey where Martin Peterson had left his launch. He returned immediately and was going to take Mrs. Forrest to Alert Bay Hospital, if she was well enough to move, or else go for the *Columbia* to come with their doctor. In this part of British Columbia there are many islands and miles and miles of coast line with no telephone, and there is no means whatever of getting in touch with the doctor at Alert Bay quickly, unless there happens to be a tugboat with wireless handy.

(August 25, 1933)

Walked along the trail with the Bennetts to the saltwater lake where Mr. Bennett is logging, and saw the A-frame boomstick borer, gasoline donkey, and a fine boom of pulpwood ready to be towed down to Powell River. Amy and Mrs. Bennett had a bathe, which they much enjoyed, it being a hot day. Supper with the Bennetts, and afterwards a three-handed cribbage session.

(August 26, 1933)

We met Martin Peterson as we were near the entrance to Port Harvey, and were very glad to hear that they got Mrs. Forrest to the hospital at Alert Bay safely on Saturday, and that she was no worse for the trip. It was foggy and as soon as the fog lifted the wind came up, so we did not continue on our way. Listened to the radio, which came in very well. Called on Mrs. Iwatha, wife of the Jap who is working with Martin. She has two cute little girls. We moved alongside some big cedar logs and made *Toketie* fast. The smell alongside some float logs is too awful for words—I think it is decayed barnacles and wood.

(August 28, 1933)

Fifty minutes to Burial Cove, where we had lunch. Afterwards went ashore and visited Mr. and Mrs. Jamieson, and her sister-in-law. They have a very nice place. Later we crossed Havannah

Channel and anchored opposite the deserted Indian village Matilpi. On the burial island opposite it, skulls and bones lie jumbled about on the ground, surrounded by old coffin boxes, some tied with cedar bark rope, but all are open and no bones in them, evidently been looted. The burial house has tumbled down and boards lie about among the bones. The coffin boxes are nailed and some sewn with sinew, but they are not carved, nor the sides made out of one piece of cedar.

(July 22, 1933)

Chopped our way through the undergrowth to the only remaining standing door frame, with a huge house beam, round and carved, lying by it on the ground. The machete I brought along is the clear thing for chopping away underbrush, as it cuts very small stuff as well as fairly big. Amy got busy hunting round the platform of the old lodge site, finding two beads up to date, while I took a photo of the house beam for Bill Newcombe, to compare with his photo of 1900. The house beam I photographed today was 53 feet long and 30 inches in diametre.

(August 12, 1934)

Went over to Hat Island and got two specimens of flatheads for the National Museum, Ottawa. Tied up at the Jamieson's float. Amy made some delicious jelly as we came along, of wild gooseberries, which we just picked. She added a little rhubarb and lemon. The Jamiesons were away when we arrived but returned later. They had been to a party at Potts Lagoon and lost the tide through the narrows and had to wait. In the evening we all went in *Toketie* to Chatham Channel and had supper with the Adderleys. They have a splendid garden and grow vegetables and flowers, but at present he is crippled considerably, one of his legs giving him great pain from an old war wound, and he cannot get a pension.

(August 11, 1935)

We had dinner with the Jamiesons and at 2.45 we all left in *Toketie* for Bones Cannery. While we were there a packer came in from Kingcome Inlet with 1000 humpbacks and cohoes. We went to supper with the manager, Mr. Dorman, and his wife. During the time we were there all these salmon were canned. Last week one day they put up 2300 cases in 14 hours, a record for the cannery. I saw the machinery for canning salmon in operation but was just too late to see the Iron Chink working.

(August 14, 1935)

J. G. (Jack) Dorman selected the Bones Bay site in 1927, supervised the construction of the huge edifice set on pilings, and then stayed to manage the Canadian Fish Company cannery for all of its operating years. In its heyday the plant employed 85 Chinese, more than 100 Indian women and more than 100 fishermen. In 1949 the cannery was closed and all the canning equipment removed, although the buildings were still used as storage sheds for nets.

Got a few things at the Minstrel Id. store and filled up with gas and coal oil. Mr. H. C. Northcote, of Cracroft Id., the late local fishery warden, came and had a yarn and lunch with us. He has been in these parts 40 years, and gave us useful information about tides locally. He has a collection of Indian things at his home at Cracroft, and asked us to call in there on our way down and see it. He says the Indians living on Village Id. have shown him their ceremonial things which are hidden away and shown to very few white people. Cabeen was up to his eyes in numerous jobs so there was no chance of his straightening the propeller blades today. The *Columbia* came in and I got them to send me *The Log of the Columbia* for some time to come. I had a yarn with a fisherman at the store. He told me that in Call Creek at the very low tides one can get rock oysters about a foot long, and on one occasion he filled a washtub with twelve. Judging by those we found in Gorge Harbour I have no reason to doubt this statement. He said in Drew Harbour there are also very big ones, but of quite a different shape. Both kinds are very good eating.

(August 13, 1934)

Minstrel Island was the social and business hub of the area. The settlement, crowded around a small indentation in the Minstrel Island shore, had a general store, marine gas stations, hotel, post office, machine shop, laundry, café, pool room and pub. It was famous for lengthy and very rough drinking parties.

The early mornings are very foggy in these parts, but by 10 o'clock the sun generally comes out and the rest of the day is perfect. Amy cut my hair this morning on the beach at Matilpi, with nail scissors and very tweaky clippers. It was a very painful proceeding but successful. Cabeen said if we went on the skids at 4.30 A.M. tomorrow he would attend to the propeller when the tide went down. Mr. Knowles arrived shortly after we did. He ran the store last year, but now travels round in his boat and sells Watkins Products to people up the coast. We went on his boat and he showed us face powder, hand cleanser, shaving soap, spices, custard powder etc. etc. We expended $5 on his goods and afterwards he came to lunch with us. Young Halliday is running the store and gas station, and Neil Hood attends to the beer-parlour and post office.

(August 15, 1934)

Put *Toketie* on the skids at 4.30 A.M. and after breakfast rowed down the narrow channel between Minstrel Id. and Cracroft Id. to a splendid midden and house-site about 50 yards long. The beach has a plentiful sprinkling of empty beer bottles owing to its proximity to the beer parlor close by. During the morning Cabeen took off the propeller and straightened the blades. We were very lucky. There is good metal in the propeller and the shaft was not too bent and the gum-wood false keel showed no signs of bumping on the rocks at Estero Basin. Cabeen told us of a pictograph close to Minstrel Id. on the mainland shore, about a mile from the wharf. We set out in *Toketie* to photograph it, but I took photos with difficulty owing to the steepness of the rocks. Amy found another picto about 100 yards away. I had to leave one group as I could neither sketch nor photo it, owing to bushes growing in front of it.

(August 16, 1934)

Cabeen kindly came over with us to the bluff and climbed up and cut away some bushes. I did not feel equal to scaling the rocks. On arriving back at Minstrel Id., met Halliday, who came on board for a chat. It was boat day, and later on there would be crowds of boats, and people going to the store and beer-parlor. We were very pleased to find Jim Stanton at the float. He had arrived a few minutes before us, from the head of Knight Inlet, and was taking out his Easthope engine and hoped to replace it with a Vivian engine which was on the float, and which had come up from Vancouver by the last boat. Jim and his friend came to lunch with us, and afterwards returned to

their work of getting out the old engine. We left for Lagoon
Cove, as there is a dance tonight at Minstrel Id which I understand will go on till tomorrow and much beer and ice cream
flow.

(August 11, 1939)

Lagoon Cove. Anchored for the night in front of Alex Far-
quharson's house. We went ashore and had a yarn with Mr. and
Mrs. Farquharson, known to everyone as the Scottys. They
later came on board and talked, and listened to the radio.
Scotty is logging a mile or more up the river at the head of
Thompson Sound and comes home on Saturday till Monday.
He traps in the winter.

Found a horizontal hammer stone on the Scotty's beach and
Mrs. Scotty gave us a black stone hammer which they had
found on their place. Went across the cove to a circular small
island where "Snowey" has his garden, but the gate was locked
and "Snowey" away prospecting, so we could not look at the
midden. Some boat came in recently and the people pinched
some of his vegetables, hence the lock on the gate. The island,
like so many in this part of the world, was covered with midden, a lot of wild rose bushes where it had not been cleared.
"Snowey" has found a good many artifacts while digging. He
has wonderful vegetables. In a part of the province like this,
where people are a hundred miles or more from a butcher, one
regrets that the government should be so assinine as to pass a
law that the bottling of venison is illegal. This is bad enough,
but when they take off the bounty on cougar and wolves, which
are destroying countless deer, and chasing them out of the
many districts where they used to be plentiful, one wonders
whether the people who are responsible for these pitiful laws
can be sane.

(August 21, 1933)

Perhaps they would have gone up Knight Inlet anyway, for they
had explored the other mainland inlets and arms, and Knight Inlet
is only the longest and loneliest. However, an invitation to visit Jim
Stanton and see the famous grizzly bears was welcome indeed.
When the snows are melting, all 60 miles of Knight Inlet have
countless waterfalls spilling down the mountains that rise thou-

sands of feet from the water's edge. Usually a current runs out of the inlet due to the quantity of fresh water escaping to the ocean. Anchorages and shelters are few but overnight moorage can be found in small coves where the bow and stern can be fastened to trees. The two safe stopover places are Glendale and Wahshihlas Bay. The *Toketie* stopped first at Glendale.

Jim Stanton finished up his job with the new engine, and we all started off at 1.45 P.M. We had a nice run up the Inlet to Glendale Cove. Anchored for the night.

(August 2, 1935)

Between Kwalate Point and Herries Point we saw three pictographs. We crossed to the east side of the Inlet and looked for the pictograph between Bald Peak and Tsukola Point but could not find it. At Cascade Point we stopped for a few moments and I took a photo of the two waterfalls. We ran up to Wahshihlas Bay, looking for the black pictograph at Hatchet Point, which however we were unable to find. The Stantons came into Wahshihlas Bay where we had anchored to wait for them and we then ran up to the slough where the Stantons have their house, they giving us the lead in. They live about two miles from the river mouth.

(August 3, 1935)

We had a very comfortable night and were wakened by blue jays chattering everywhere and the Stantons' big dog walking over our cabin top, anxious to wag tails with our dogs. The Stantons have a little cabin on the back of the slough, and there is always depth enough of water where we are tied up for boats, about 50 yards from their home. There is long grass right across the river flat where the grizzlies spend their time now, digging roots. Stanton says they often cross the slough where we are, and yesterday, coming up, their dog winded one, close by. Stanton says he has watched two grizzlies for some years here, who spend most of their time boxing and wrestling, and it is a comical sight. They often come quite close. We are tied astern of Don Munday's boat, he and his party being up in the mountains. Stanton is a guide and packer, and has a long, flat punt for taking stuff up the river, and he puts a kicker on it or poles it. He took in the Munday party about a week ago, taking over half a ton of supplies up the river in the punt. As soon as he got back home, news came of the Dean Brock fatality, and he had to turn round and make the trip back again to the mountains and bring out one of Dean Brock's sons, who was with the Munday party.

(August 4, 1935)

Don and Phyllis Munday, British Columbia's foremost mountaineers, climbed more of the province's mountains than anyone else, exploring and mapping the Coast Range. This was pioneer country for climbers when the Mundays began their mapping work during the 1920s. Few mountains were even named. "Waddington was called Mystery Mountain as no one knew exactly where it was," Phyllis once remarked.[1] Mount Waddington, rising 13,280 feet into the clouds, is the coast's highest peak, and was climbed three times by the Mundays without their achieving the summit. Not until their fourth attempt did they reach the second peak of this giant. The Mundays also studied glaciers, recorded mountain flora and organized mountain rescue work. Don Munday, a shy, quiet man, described well the business of mountaineering in his book *The Unknown Mountain*, written just before his death in 1950. Mount Munday was named to honour this intrepid couple.

Dean R. W. Brock and his wife Mildred died in an air crash at the end of July 1935. A Boeing flying boat had stopped at Alta Lake to pick up Mrs. Brock, who was staying at their summer camp, and had then failed to gain altitude on takeoff. Brock was one of Canada's foremost geologists, at one time Deputy Minister of Mines for Canada, and at the time of his death Dean of the Faculty of Applied Science at the University of British Columbia, President of the Royal Society of Canada and Chairman of the Vancouver Harbours Board. Mildren (Britten) Brock, a warm, outgoing woman, frequently opened her beautiful home and gardens to support good causes. Brock House is still used for such purposes.

We have only to dip a bucket overboard to get fresh water. It is glaciated and a bit muddy but it soon settles. This will do old *Toketie* good as she has green whiskers on her. The Stantons, like ourselves, are fond of animals, and they have two black cats and a dog, and a pig which has not appeared. The only grizzly that really bothered them got too friendly and used to come

round the house and would not get out of their way, and as
Stanton is away often and his wife alone here, he thought it better to kill it.

(August 3, 1935)

After lunch we all piled into the Stanton's punt, putting Munday's skiff across the bows and our Johnson propelled us down
to Dutchman's Head where Stanton is getting a cabin built.
After leaving some grub for a young fellow and his wife there,
we went on up various sloughs, crossed the main river and into
another slough where we left Don Munday's skiff for the party
to use when they get out of the mountains. There were holes
everywhere where the grizzlies had been digging up roots. We
landed at the Indian village and saw the oolichan pits, fire
places and wooden tanks which were stored in a hut. Grizzly
tracks were everywhere. We found the Stantons' pig rooting
round at the village. We returned to the Stantons' slough and
they had supper with us. After supper Stanton climbed 150 feet
up his observation tree, from which he can see all over the flats.
He said there were two grizzlies about 200 yards from us, but if
we went down the slough in the punt to the place, we would
have to land to see them. One he recognized as being a bad
actor, as he had always chased anyone away who had ever gone
near him, so we did not take any chances.

(August 4, 1935)

The eulachon (spelling variations include oolachon, hollikan, oli-
gan etc.) site, deserted when the Stantons and the Barrows were
there in mid-summer, would have been busy indeed in March,
when the eulachon arrived. The small, silvery, smelt-like fish, mi-
grating in countless millions, were eagerly awaited, and caused an
explosion of activity. The eulachon came first to the north, as early
as February, but the people at Knight Inlet might not welcome
them until March, and the fish only reached the Fraser in April or
May. Scooped from the sea in nets made of nettle fibre, the fish
were then placed in pits in the ground, which the Barrows observed. After decomposing for about ten days, they were put into
the wooden vats and hot stones were dropped in, to boil the water
in the vats. The rising oil was scooped out and bottled in kelp
gourds or small wooden boxes with lids. The smell of ripening eu-

lachon was strong enough, but the oil attained an even more powerful stench. The Indian people, who enjoyed the flavour, dipped fish, roasted roots and other foods into the oil. To eat berries without a coating of eulachon oil was to be poor indeed. The oil was traded long distances, over routes known as grease trails.

I notice people here carry a rifle whenever they do any travelling by land, as a precaution, for grizzly tracks are everywhere. Stanton and I sawed a piece of maple he had got to make a pair of snow shoes, or rather bear paws. Freddy Short arrived and he and Stanton worked at Freddy's Easthope engine, putting in some gaskets as the bearings were too tight. Then all three of us tried to make Mrs. Short's old-time Singer sewing machine sew, but all it did was to punch holes in the material. The Stantons came to supper with us and later the Shorts joined us. The no-see-ums were pretty bad and we made a smudge of Amy's old pyjamas and let them smoulder in the frying pan in the cockpit, which made things better. We also lit a candle in the cabin and hundreds of the pests flew into the flame.

(August 6, 1935)

Most of the heroic people of the Inside Coast are unknown. Jim and Laurette Stanton are exceptions, for their adventurous lives at the head of Knight Inlet are recorded in Beth Day's book, *Grizzlies in their Backyard*. Born in Snohomish, Washington, in 1885, Jim was orphaned when very young and grew up in a series of homes. Rheumatic fever left him undersized; "a mean little devil, always itching for a fight" is how he described himself.[2] From the age of nine, he spent a few winters with an old Norwegian trapper, helping him on the trapline. This did not help his schooling, and when he was 15 he was expelled. Laurette also was orphaned early in life, and when she and Jim met they found they had something else in common: the powerful dream of an escape into the wilderness. Jim built up a successful garage business in Seattle, but the dream would not go away. Finally they sold everything, bought a boat and supplies, and headed north. Along the way, exploring among the islands for the place that felt right to them, they heard tales of the grizzlies of Knight Inlet and discovered that this was their destination. At Wahshihlas Bay, they found an abandoned trapper's cabin and moved in. They laid out 15 miles of trapline, for Jim hoped to get $33 per marten skin and eight dollars for mink, but when they sold their pelts the following year they were devastated to discover that in the post-First World War slump, marten skins brought only four dollars and prime mink were worth $1.50. They saw their dream of living in the wilderness collapsing.

However, in that spring of 1920 two hand-loggers arrived: Tommy Bartlett and his Swedish partner Martin Petersen (whom the Barrows met at Port Harvey). Bachelors, they towed in a well-furnished house-float run by a motherly housekeeper, Mrs. Forrest (the lady who was taken ill at Forward Bay in 1933). They wanted Jim to work for them and he was desperate enough to agree. At the end of the summer they had 150,000 feet of cedar which in the spring had been worth $44 for 1000 feet. Just before the three men got their cedar to a buyer, the market dropped and the best they could get was $7.50 per thousand. Jim earned only $300.

Instead of heading back for Seattle, the Stantons decided to try commercial fishing, trolling for coho. The following year they fished with a gillnetter, in the days when the 1200-foot nets had to be managed by hand. In 1924 they moved to the head of the inlet, where the Barrows visited them. They built more traplines, with overnight cabins along them. Slowly, their dogged hard work and persistence yielded results. Jim gained a reputation as big-game and fishing guide and yachts began to arrive at their dock. One of the biggest yachts was the *Surprise*, 255 feet long, from whose owner Jim bought for Laurette the piano in the lounge.

After Laurette's death in 1961, Jim lived in Victoria for a time but he soon headed back to Knight Inlet. Back amid the towering snowy peaks, in the familiar log house, he could look from his door across the flats of the rip-roaring Klinaklini River, watch the grizzlies feeding like cattle or wrestling playfully and hear their gigantic snores. There he lived until his death in 1978 at the age of 93.

> Laurette, Jim and I went off down the inlet to see an Indian rock painting several miles away. Not far from the mouth of the Franklyn River, as we were passing close to the shore, we saw two young grizzly, and had a good view of them for some moments as they made their way up the mountain. It was the perfect movie shot, the grizzly being in the open and the light right. Alas, I had left the movie camera behind, as I did not want it when taking photos of the pictograph.
>
> (August 18, 1939)

Jim took us all out in the punt with the 16 h.p. Johnson and we went up the Klinni Klinni River to the Indian village. We looked round, and had a good meal on the grass in front of the village. The river is very high and running swiftly. We then went off in the punt to the slough on the east side of the flat and looked at a totem which Jim had found floating down the Inlet and which he had towed to this spot. We returned in the evening after a very pleasant day. Lemon pie for supper.

(August 20, 1939)

At 4.25 P.M. we made fast to Stanton's boat and he and Mrs. S. convoyed us down the slough to deep water. Stanton told a number of grizzly yarns, but the following was one of the best. The Stantons were having supper and Mr. and Mrs. Munday were with them, when they heard one of the pigs squealing some distance away on the flats. Stanton got his rifle and ran off to see what the trouble was, and found a two-year-old cub clawing a sow and tearing her flesh with the mother grizzly sicking the cub on. Stanton shot at the cub but he was anxious not to hit the pig and he missed several times. At last he killed it and at once the mother grizzly charged him. He drew a bead on her and the rifle just clicked – no shells. He hurriedly got a box out of his pocket. The lid fell off and all the shells fell into the long grass. The grizzly was right up to him by now and Stanton got hold of the barrel to use his rifle as a club. The grizzly took a swipe at him, but at that moment the pig ran right by them and the grizzly tried to swipe it. She then ran after the pig for 50 yards or so, and Stanton hurriedly searched in the long grass for his shells. By good luck he found one, put it in the rifle, and as the grizzly charged him again he shot her in the neck and she came down dead. Mrs. Stanton put tar into the sow's deep wounds (they could see her back bone) and she soon recovered and produced thirteen piglets.

(August 7, 1935)

Good-bye to our kind friends. A mile north of Herries Pt. on the other side of the inlet, Amy spotted the picto we missed going up, and we stopped and took a photo of it. We then crossed to the shore between Herries Point and Kwalate Point and in this area found no less than five groups of pictos which I photographed and sketched. We moved on toward Naena Point.

Two miles north of Naena Point we had to run slow. All our clothes in the cabin and the bedding got soaked, the spray coming in under the windows. Old *Toketie* behaved very well and the engine purred along in its accustomed style. Windows such as we have are not the best for a small boat in windy weather as they are bound to let water in. We found more sea than we liked running at Naena Point, so we went across to the bay opposite the cannery in Glendale Cove. We anchored among the gill-netters.

(August 23, 1939)

I talked to some of the fishermen and gathered that it is pretty windy everywhere, so much so that some of them did not fish. The day was sunny and dried out our clothes in the wind. At one gust of wind, nearly all the boats dragged anchor, ours included, and there was much put-putting of engines as we got back again.

(August 24, 1939)

We went over to the cannery and saw Mr. King at the store and had a yarn with him and bought some things. He told us that on last week's boat he got 800 loaves but when we arrived they had all been sold. We had lunch at the float and afterwards made another start but returned. I am afraid I am a very poor sailor as I never know when to set out if there is wind about, and Amy's judgement is much better than mine. After our return we started off again very soon and had a good run down to Minstrel Island, which took three hours and twenty minutes. There were whitecaps everywhere but the seas were not confused and *Toketie* rode them in her usual easy way. I think this piece of water is a particularly windy spot, and the tiderips off Prominent Point make it all the worse.

(August 25, 1939)

From Minstrel Island, the Barrows went west along Clio Channel. For a week or so they explored the passages separating Harbledown, Turnour and Village Islands.

We left Lagoon Cove [near Minstrel Island] at 1.55 P.M. and running down Clio Channel there was a fresh westerly wind. We intended anchoring in the snug bay on the south side of Klaoitsis Id. but found a logging outfit taking up all the bay, so we

went on down the channel till we got into Steamer Passage, and
anchored in the east bay of Hazel Id. About 4 o'clock when we
were having tea, ten U.S.A. Army planes flew over our heads
on their way back from visiting Alaska. At 8.35 P.M. the Province
News Reporter stated they had arrived at Seattle earlier in the
evening. After tea we rowed among this group of small islands
to Harbledown Id., where we landed on a fine midden. It was
high tide, but Amy found a chisel and I a horizontal hammer,
quite a good specimen. This place is or was called in Indian,
Lulaladsi, the dead body ground, owing to there being many
burial mounds on the small islands, some with large fantastic
figures of killer whales, made of boards, guarding the dead.

(August 17, 1934)

At 10.30 A.M. we went over to Nicholas Pt. near Karlukwees Village and I took photos of the pictographs. David Williams, one
of the Indians living at the village, made his gas boat fast to *Toketie* and came on board. We then anchored in the bay in front
of Karlukwees village and I took a lot of photos of totems, and
one of Mrs. David Williams and Mrs. Wilson. Charley, a little
Indian boy, was much interested in my photographic efforts.
Before we left we traded a can of cherries for a can of oolichan
oil and bought a small totem, about 4 feet high and minus a leg
and arms, for $1. Amy found some beads etc. on the beach,
while I was photographing. We left about 5.30 and anchored in
Oien's Bay, Village Island, for the night. Mr. Oien's little farm is
in a bay S.E. of the Indian village, Mamalilaculla. Mr. Oien is of
Scandinavian extraction and Mrs. Oien from Scotland. Her
father was factor for many years to the late Lord Roseberry.
They have two cows and a nice garden which produces splendid stuff, the soil being clam shell midden like ours at home;
but getting more rain in the summer than we do, the things
grow even better than with us. The Oiens have a ready sale for
everything they can produce, among the logging camps, both in
winter and summer. They sell milk, butter, cream, eggs, logan-
berries and strawberries, and vegetables of all kinds, & they say
there is nothing to complain about. A much more satisfactory
state of affairs with producers of farm stuff than in our part of
B.C. The Oiens came on board for a yarn, and we listened to

the radio till after midnight. The reception seems to be very good here or else it was a good night for the radio.

(August 19, 1934)

Went ashore after breakfast and looked at the Oien's cows pulling a stoneboat. They are very quiet in harness and ploughed up the clover field before it was sown. They are great pets and give a lot of milk, Holstein Jersey cross. Poor Rinnie suddenly screamed with pain & we found him caught in a bear trap. Amy and I ran to try & get him out and got bitten a bit, but Mr. Oien soon had the clamps on the trap and we got the poor little fellow out. Fortunately his paws were not caught near the centre of the trap but at the side where it did not close quite tight and this saved any bones being broken. Except for a bad pinch and the shock, old Rinnie escaped any further damage I am thankful to say. After lunch we went in the rowboat to Mamalilaculla or Mimkumlees and saw Miss O'Brien the missionary there. We looked over the village & I took some photos of totems. In the evening we went ashore & spent the evening with the Oiens.

(August 12, 1933)

From 1900 to 1945, Miss Kathleen O'Brien and her friend, Kate Dibben, were missionaries to the Indians. Leaving English society life "to get away from tea parties", Miss O'Brien with her own money built the small sanatorium called "Lyuyatsi", meaning Resting Place; apart from a $400 annual grant from the Women's Auxiliary of the Church of England and the generosity of her friends, she supported the mission work herself.[3] With her encouragement the Indians built a fine church from which a bell rang on Sundays to call them to worship. In 1945 the Department of Indian Affairs took over Indian education and the two women returned to England. Kathleen O'Brien won recognition on the King's Honours List and remained in England, but Kate Dibben returned to the British Columbia coast, where she died in 1955.

Visiting Mamalilaculla about 35 years later, Doras Kirk found that the village had been vandalized. No one lived there, and most of the houses had been ransacked. In the O'Brien Memorial School, the plumbing and electrical wiring had been ripped out. Many totem poles, half rotting, lay buried in the blackberries. Almost hidden in the brush, a single cedar log, about four feet in diameter and 30 feet long, had been smoothed and chiselled in readiness for raising. Abruptly the new civilization of the white people had arrived and the adzed beam was never raised.

At Mamalilaculla we met Miss O'Brien and two ladies staying with her. She showed us her little hospital for T.B. patients and there is now a little Indian girl of 10 there, the relation of the chief of Karlukwees village who died last year. Her name is Christine. We saw the small totems that the Indian Agent Todd thought we wanted but they did not look very interesting. The totem with the sad face and tall hat that I took a photo of three years ago, the Indian boys rolled down the bank into the sea after uprooting it last Hallowe'en night. We saw a fluted house beam that was half sawn up for fire wood. I took some photos of totems and the ladies gave us afternoon tea.

(July 31, 1935)

Visited the Oiens. They asked us to their mid-day meal which we much enjoyed. They showed us the rhubarb I sent them last fall, which has established itself very well. After dinner I helped Oien turn hay, which the cows later hauled to the barn. I changed the oil in the crank case and then helped Oien put the hay in the barn. We had supper with the Oiens which included one of Mrs. Oien's famed sausage pies with custard filling. This was a meal that should be recorded.

(August 13, 1936)

The Oiens came to lunch with us on board, and Mrs. Oien interested us with her experiences when she was Matron in an Industrial School in Glasgow. We raked up hay again, and after Oien and I had put it in the barn, he, Amy and I took his 28-foot cannery skiff over to Tsatsichnukwomi with the aid of *Toketie*. John Bull was on the beach and Ed had no trouble catching him. He tied him up and gave him a feed. We looked in the old lodge to see if the two old dishes we saw there some years ago were still there. They were not, and I am afraid we have lost the chance of getting them, which is too bad. John Bull is a fine beast, quite docile, and he walked onto the skiff without any bother. The house totem, that I photographed last year, and his partner, were both lying in the nettles, the house in front of them having been cleared away. These house totems, in all their glory, and supporting the house beams, were photographed in 1900 by Dr. Newcombe, with the chiefs in their ceremonial robes in front. Amy could find none of the old muskets she noticed last time, lying about, among the sand and clam shell on the beach.

(July 31, 1935)

I went over to Mamalilaculla with Ed, who had to deliver milk and berries at the village. Miss Dibben was quite busy, cooking, looking after Miss O'Brien who had the 'flu and a temperature, and holding a service at the same time, it being Sunday. We returned and had lunch at the Oiens, the piece de resistance being coffee cream. In the afternoon, Amy, Ed and I went over to Mrs. Jolliffe's on Harbledown Id. in *Toketie*. The object of the visit was to find out where the two dishes we saw some years ago at Tsatsichnukwomi were, and we found that they are now in Victoria, so our chance of getting them has vanished. Before going over, Ed and I hauled in the last of the hay, little John (Ferdinand) Bull hauling it on the sleigh, which he accomplished with very little effort. Visited the store kept by Mr. Jolliffe's brother-in-law and was able to get some Millbank cigarettes which I had been out of for some days.

(August 29, 1939)

Went to the village of New Vancouver. I don't think the Indians use it much. Had a walk round the beaches and fed an Indian dog that was holding down the village by himself. There are two canoes about 50 feet long and 3 feet deep pulled up on the beach out of the sun. They must have made them out of fine cedars but they had seen better days. There were a few community houses & not many totems, but those there were very interesting, & possibly older than at Mimkumlees. Amy got a couple of brass bracelets & the usual collection of trade beads. Mrs. Jolliffe, a Kanaker, brought us a bunch of roses and onions before we left our anchorage.

(August 15, 1933)

Mrs. Jolliffe was one of the two daughters of Kamano, a Hawaiian who was also Harbledown Island's first foreign settler. The other daughter married Mr. Olney, who had the first oxen team to log the island. Mr. Jolliffe owned a steam tug used to tow booms to market. He also fished, first as a gillnetter, then in a salmon and herring seiner, and finally as a halibut long-liner.

From Old Vancouver we went through White Beach Passage into Blackfish Sound and almost to the W. end of Hanson Id. The day was perfect & we could see the distant mountains on Vancouver Id. and beyond Drury Inlet very clearly. Had we wished to see Alert Bay, today would have been the right day, or to travel up Queen Charlotte Strait. But Alert Bay with modern Indian houses does not appeal to us. We trolled back by way of Farewell Harbour and anchored in a snug little bay by Mound Id. & went ashore & explored a small terraced village site with plenty of midden. I was astonished to find a spearhead & chisel on the beach. In these parts there is plenty of midden but artifacts are remarkably scarce. Then we went over to a bay by Mink Point on Turnour Id. and anchored for the night. There has been a small settlement in this bay & the usual deep midden. XER the Mexican station is coming in very loud on the radio tonight. The engineer on the *Columbia* told me rather an interesting thing about reception. He said some little while ago they were coming north about 7.30 in the morning through Seymour Narrows and the radio was coming in remarkably well. As soon as they got through the Narrows it stopped all of a sudden, just as if it had been shut off by a wall, and he has always noticed it to be better south of that place.

(August 15, 1933)

Went by Johnson to the end of Canoe Passage between Village Id. and Turnour Id., a mass of kelp from the narrowest spot right to the Knight Inlet end, but we managed to dodge it & only once get kelp round the propeller. There is a lot of midden at the narrow spit on the Village Id. side. We did not get back to *Toketie* & lunch till 3, and as we were having it, Oien came alongside in his gasboat & gave us a pan of peas from his garden. He was on his way to Harbledown Id. to give mail to a neighbour who is going up to Minstrel Id. tomorrow, steamer day. At 4.15 we left for Klaoitsis Id. which place we reached after 1 hour & 5 minutes. We are in a snug bay sheltered by Cracroft Id and a unnamed island at the end of Baronet Passage. We found a spring on the beach, filled up with decaying leaves

and mud. I got busy and cleaned it out. The water came into
the basin pretty fast and I think tomorrow we can have a washing day here. Klaoitsis Island was inhabited by Indians at one
time, and there is lots of midden in this bay. I noticed a burial
site at the west end, with a big wooden killer whale painted in
black and white. The dogs put up a big grouse here this evening. We do not like them to roam in the woods much on account of the wolves. The latter have been the cause of the dis-
appearance of several local dogs, and Oien lost a calf owing to
them. I noticed wolf & deer tracks on the mud on the beach
this morning.

(August 16, 1933)

The spring was quite clear this morning and full up to the top,
beautiful water. We did a 40-piece wash. When I say "we", I did
4 out of the 40. The sun is very hot today & the clothes will not
take long to dry on the cod line. At 2.45 we left for Karlukwee's
Village. Amy picked up some beads on the beach and fragments
of stone things & I took more photos. There was not a soul
there today. The large totem that I took a photo of a year or
two ago is now lying on the ground and the Hoh hoh totem that
I photographed last year has now only one wing. So it goes, till
at last they rot.

(August 17, 1933)

Doras Kirk in 1974 described a later stage in this sad process. A
single totem with a gooseberry bush like wild hair growing from its
crown stood guard in Karlukwees. Annabelle and Basil Anders
came to harvest fruit from the old orchards but otherwise the village was silent in the heat. "When I was a boy there were totems all
along the waterfront," Basil told Doras Kirk. "Now they are all
gone to museums, or people come in by boat and just take them."[4]

It rained a bit in the night, which was not very good for our
washing hanging out to dry. However a few more hours of sun
will dry it, and the day looks as if it might improve. We got up
late & had breakfast of bacon and eggs: the eggs of the case variety, which we got at the Minstrel Id. store some time ago, are
not pleasant enough to boil now. It is just noon, and Amy has
rowed ashore in her birthday suit for a bathe. This would be a
splendid place to dodge pressing creditors. There are so many
narrow channels and small islands dotted about everywhere.

The glass has gone up two points since yesterday. We had a dandy stew for supper, stewed prunes and tapioca. Amy went off fishing and I did some more coloured sketches of pictographs. As I make three of each, one for Harlan Smith, one for W. A. Newcombe and one for myself, there are a good many to do. The ship's clock stopped today, a tragedy that happened also to Vancouver on his voyage to the North Pacific, and he got away with it, and I hope we shall. I suppose no-see-ums have got into the works, as they did last year, but how they get in is more than I can say. We got in the washing. One towel had blown into the spring but that did not matter very much. At night we listened to the Hollywood Bowl concert which finished up with Negro music. The reception might have been better, but it might have been much worse. Speaking of lagoons, one thing we have discovered on this trip is not to anchor near the mouth of any that go inland for any distance and have deep water in them. We have been warned several times about this & told that there are considerable overfalls at the mouths of some of them. At Mackenzie Sound there was one spot called the "Roaring Hole", the mouth of one of these places.

(August 19, 1933)

We went for a few miles along Beware Passage to the Pedersen's camp on Harbledown Id. and were pleased to meet them again. After Peggy had got the men their dinner, she came on board for a chat, and later on I took photos of Peggy and her husband. Peggy recently got her 18-year-old son out from Scotland and she says he is so Scotch she can't understand a word he says, although she is Scotch too. Peggy gave us a pie which she baked for us while we were there, some bottled crabmeat and some cake.

(August 14, 1936)

We got strawberries, raspberries, cream, milk, eggs, a big loaf of bread and vegetables from the Oiens, and after saying goodbye, we left at 11.20 A.M. and ran to Gwaestums, Gilford Id. We went on to the head of Health Bay and got information about anchoring from a logging camp. Later on we anchored just before dark in front of the old Indian village in Retreat Passage. There are a good many totems which so far we have only seen at a distance, and the modern houses are in front of the old buildings with the big cedar posts and cross beams. Amy picked up a few Hudson's Bay trade beads on the beach.

(August 8, 1933)

Went ashore and looked at the village. The old buildings, a long row of them, had nearly all carved totems supporting the huge roof beams, and in some instances the ends of the roof beams were carved. The single planks of cedar in front of the platforms round the buildings inside, were in some cases 52 feet 8 inches long by 30 inches wide and 4½ inches thick. Nettles and wild parsnip are growing thickly all round the buildings. Amy picked up a lot of old Hudson's Bay beads and a copper bracelet. I expect a lot of good stuff has been looted, as Indians are always careless in leaving everything lying about. I wish I had more plates for the camera; there are so many interesting things to take, but we will be moving on to other interesting spots and I must not use up all the plates here. I am tingling all over from having been stung by stinging nettles all day. This is not as bad as Amy, who is suffering from deer fly, no-see-ums, mosquito bites and cedar water poisoning. I expect the nettles troubled her too.

(August 9, 1933)

A note in Hilson's *Exploring Puget Sound and British Columbia* states, with reference to the chart of Gilford Island: "Old Indian village – original house posts and beams on display at the Pacific Science Center, Seattle".[5]

There are a number of coffins in the trees near the creek on the right hand side of the village. We had walked under these several times without seeing them. They are about 20 to 30 feet up the trees and some are higher up still, a cedar board above and below the coffin box. In some of the trees there are three or four coffin boxes, on branches one below the other. The long row of old lodges behind the modern houses are most interesting and in itself worth the trip here. What a sight it must have been years ago to witness a potlatch or ceremony in these buildings, with the fire burning in the centre, and the platforms all round the buildings crowded with Indians. Karlukwee's village, to the south, is interesting but it is not as big as Old Vil-

lage. There is a priceless pair of figures about 15 feet high, standing on either side of a house, with one of their arms up, each
supporting a modern barrel. They have the most comical ex-
pression, and small trees are growing out of the top of their
heads.

(August 10, 1933)

Went over to the other side of Health Bay and tied up to Mr.
McIntosh's logging float. His daughter asked us to supper, and
while we were waiting for the men to come home from work,
we went to see the old village site. Nothing remains of the
houses, but from the depth of clam shell and flat space, it must
have been a very big place. Mr. McIntosh thinks a fire must
have swept through this spit about 200 years ago, since he has
counted the rings on some of the trees he has cut down, which
number that amount, and they are growing on top of the midden. There is a fairly tall growth of trees all over the old site. In
the 1863–65 chart, Captn. Pender marks a large village at this
spot.

(August 11, 1933)

Tied up to a piece of kelp near Midsummer Id. as it was quite
foggy and the very many small islands hereabouts, some of
which are not marked on the chart, make navigation somewhat
confusing. When the fog lifted we headed for Simoom Sound.
Made fast to the Dunseith's float. They insisted on us coming to
lunch with them.

(August 29, 1939)

Just north of Echo Bay in a small inlet is the floating community
called Simoom Sound, somewhat south of the L-shaped inlet of the
same name. Because the National Film Board has made a movie
about Simoom Sound, it is the best known of the floating villages of
the coast. The community dates back to 1905, when it was just one
of many floating logging camps. During the years from about 1935
to 1941, Simoom Sound had a floating schoolhouse to serve the loggers' children from a 50-mile radius (the school children all wore
life preservers), a badminton court, houses for families, bunkhouses for bachelors, a cookhouse, workshops, storehouses, and a
bath house with stove, boiler and hot showers, all constructed on a
series of planked rafts connected by gangways. Flowers in tubs and

window boxes, and hens and chicks in wire enclosures added to the liveliness of the scene. John Dunseith's General Store was later run by his daughter.

A short run north of Simoom Sound, still on Gilford Island, is Viner Sound.

> Made fast to a boom of logs at Viner Sound. At the O'Brien booming ground I got on a boom of cedar and had a yarn with a man making up a boom close by. There were only four sections in the cedar boom but 300,000 feet of timber in it. The boom man said he had seldom seen such large logs, and I had never seen anything like them. Amy caught a nice grilse.
>
> (August 1, 1933)

Straight west along Fife Channel motored the *Toketie*, then she veered south to enter Indian Passage. In the centre of this cluster of islands is Insect Island.

> Went to Insect Id. by way of Indian Passage and tied up to Mr. McIntosh's float. McIntosh lives all alone. He used to hand log, but was stricken with paralysis all down his right side, being deaf in his right ear and blind in his right eye. He manages to use his right foot and hand a little and it is wonderful how he manages to get along. He does a little fishing and a little trapping in the winter and makes the best of his crippled condition. We had a yarn with the old man, and he showed us his garden, a very good one, in clam shell soil. After lunch we hunted in the colossal midden close by, the bank being about 15 feet high. We only found a bone point and a copper bracelet. There were evidently 3 tiers of houses at one time, but nothing left now except the flat spots where they were. The water we get now from any of the springs looks like beer but it has not got the kick. It is brown in colour. This is the cedar country. We are always pleased when we strike the clear spring water again further south. The cedar water in this part of the country poisons some people.
>
> (August 6, 1933)

Amy washed clothes, went off and caught a rock-cod which we had for lunch, and it was very good, and found a bracelet on the beach. I had a lazy morning, the only work I did being to solder McIntosh's gas can. The countless small islands at this part of the coast, all covered with cedar trees, are something well worth seeing. When one is among them it is hard to realize one is on the sea. It looks more like a vast inland lake dotted with countless islands.

(August 6, 1933)

Returning eastwards along Fife Sound, the Barrows turned north up Penphrase Passage, rounding Broughton Island, and then made an abrupt turn eastwards to enter Kingcome Inlet. Barrow had met Halliday of Kingcome Inlet on the wharf at Minstrel Island, where young Halliday ran the store, so it is not surprising to find the Barrows on their way to visit these new friends at their remote homestead.

We left for the head of Kingcome Inlet arriving at the river mouth without any untoward event. We had some difficulty however at the river mouth in finding the channel. Leaving *Toketie* at the mouth, we johnsoned up to Mr. Halliday's for information. We went back and ran *Toketie* up to his float. Later Mr. Halliday and his son came down and we had a yarn.

(July 30, 1933)

Helped load hay during the morning. Mr. Halliday has splendid fields by the river. He has a fairly big herd of cows, and the Union Steamship Co. takes all the butter he can send them. Potatoes and things of that ilk he sells to the logging camps. I notice blue lupins growing all along the river bank. At 4 P.M. Mrs. Halliday came with us in the rowboat, Johnson propelling, to see the Indian village about a mile further up the river. There are a lot of totems along the street of houses, some however being quite modern. There is quite an elaborate painted totem, quite modern, over a grave some little distance from the village. I took photos of 2 old totems and of an oval granite boulder with a carved face on it. It was an interesting trip. We johnsoned Mrs. Halliday to within a short distance of her home, up a narrow backwater, trees growing over the water each side. This channel can only be used at high tide. People from the *Columbia*, tied to a boom at the entrance to the river, visited the Hallidays in the evening. They call every fortnight.

(July 31, 1933)

Kingcome Inlet is a place known to thousands. Not only are the Hallidays of Kingcome a famous pioneer family, but the Indian life of the inlet has been sensitively described by Margaret Craven in her book *I Heard the Owl Call my Name*.

Up this inlet in the fall of 1893, three young men sailed and rowed a small sloop. They were brothers Ernest and William Halliday and their brother-in-law, Harry Kirby. Setting out from Comox to examine the head of Kingcome Inlet as a possible homestead site, they found what they were looking for: hundreds of acres of natural meadowland on the river flats. They built a log cabin and stayed through the winter to judge the severity of the cold weather. There were friendly Indian people at the village farther upstream, but the nearest white settlement was Alert Bay, 60 miles away.

Next year Ernest paid the captain of a small steamer (engaged in freighting stone blocks from Haddington Island to Victoria for the building of the new government building) to bring in his wife Lilly Elizabeth, their children, their household effects, and four oxen, two cows and a bull. They moved into the 17- by 28-foot log cabin, and there they lived for 35 years. A smaller cabin was later built nearby for the sons, as they grew up. Eighteen months after her arrival, during which time she had not seen another white woman, Lilly Elizabeth decided to return to Comox to have her third child. It was a bitterly cold December and the tiny rowboat was crowded, with two men, one woman, two children, a dog and the necessary supplies. The trip took 14 days; part of the time was spent stormbound in the warmth of Indian villages. However, although all survived the trip and the new baby was healthy and strong, Lilly Halliday had her next two children at Kingcome Inlet. Her last two children were born at Comox, at a time when better transportation was available. Of her seven children, two died of tuberculosis, but the other five have stayed on the coast: Dorothy (Mrs. Jack Macdonald), James R. Halliday who took over the farm, Roy Harry Halliday, Jean (Mrs. L. G. Duggan) and Ernest Jr. Ernest Halliday's brother William, an Indian Agent for 38 years, was involved in the trial which followed Dan Cranmer's illegal potlatch of 1921, when the heirlooms of various Kwakiutl families were surrendered.

For the first 17 years, Ernest Halliday made a monthly trip by rowboat to Alert Bay, a four-day exercise, to sell his beef at ten cents a pound. The day came when he had a profit of $28 to splurge, so he bought Lilly a six-foot kitchen cabinet. Lilly never forgot the day she saw her husband wearily rowing towards her with a huge piece of topheavy furniture laid across the rowboat.

Growing markets brought prosperity and by 1927 there were other settlers as well: Harry Kirby, with a fine farm across the river from the Hallidays, the Lansdowne family, and Mr. Jackson the retired sailor. B. A. McKelvie, writing in *The Province* in 1927, explained that Halliday built dykes to protect his fields from high spring and autumn tidal flooding. In that year the Hallidays sold more than two tons of butter to the logging camps and to the boats that came up the inlet. By the time of the Barrow visit, the Hallidays occupied a modern ten-room house, with a wide porch, surrounded by Lilly's garden, a tangle of roses, sweetpeas and many other flowers. The old Morris and Heath *Marine Atlas of the Northwest* appears to issue a general invitation: "Visitors are always welcome at the R. E. Halliday's farm, two miles upriver."[6]

> After breakfast went up to the Hallidays and bought some farm produce from them, butter, meat, cream, milk and vegetables. After saying good-bye we went down the river and made *Toketie* fast to the boom near the mouth. We then johnsoned about a quarter of a mile up the river and I took a photo of the totem standing on the bank. It is a modern antique, but its setting is quite fine, in the flat marsh land, with the snow-capped mountains in the distance. We then johnsoned about a quarter of a mile beyond *Toketie* down the inlet and I sketched some modern pictographs which were quite amusing. There were representation of "coppers" in red. The "coppers" denote the wealth of the Indians. To the right of these, in black paint, there were eleven cattle, purchased from Mr. Halliday in 1927, when the local Indians gave a big potlatch. In another group there were two coppers and a sailing ship. From an archaeological point of view they are of little interest.
>
> (August 1, 1933)

Westward down Kingcome Inlet went the Barrows, and westward along Sutlej Channel to poke into Claydon Bay, Drury Inlet and finally into Mackenzie Sound, the most northerly of their ports of call.

> Claydon Bay, Grappler Sound. We got a warm welcome from the Reynolds. I took some movies in the morning of the float-

house garden and we went to lunch with the Reynolds. After
supper went across the bay to see Toby Bergs, where we spent
the evening.

(August 30, 1939)

We were reluctant to say good-bye to our hospitable friends.
We left for O'Brien Bay on Kinnaird Id., where we got gas at
the store. We then went on to the Indian village at Hopetown
Passage, but as the Indians were there we were unable to hunt
round, so we had lunch.

(August 31, 1939)

Left for Drury Inlet, Mr. Scott and his wife, who we met earlier
in the morning, giving us the lead through in their launch. It
was quite swirly especially at the part where the rock is in the
centre of the channel. We then ran to Bedwell Point. Then we
crossed the Inlet to the Scott's float and made fast to the boom.
It is a boiling hot day. Black flies are bad here. They are the
devil and even attack *me*. The Scotts and their partner and his
wife and little boy came on board in the evening and listened to
the radio. Towards midnight a pack of wolves came down to
the beach within a hundred feet of *Toketie* and made an awful
racket howling. We could see their eyes with the flashlight. It
was a warning to us not to let Rinnie and Nannie stray far from
us. After our radio and wolf concert, we had a nice quiet night.
We shut the windows to keep out the infernal black-fly, and to
keep Rinnie and Nannie from jumping through the window
and getting ashore on the boom logs. This morning we found
that the pack of wolves last night were just at the end of the
boom stick on shore, that we were made fast to. They came to
try to make a meal of our dogs, or they chose that spot to howl
at the full moon. The various keys in which the wolves howled
showed that there were quite a number there. They were an-
swered by a pack not far off. After breakfast we rowed to an old
Indian village site about half a mile east of the Scott's float.
There were old fishtraps at this bay. At 11.35 we left the Scott's
float, they giving us a bunch of sweet-peas grown on the float,
and the partner giving us a bottle of prawns which we had for
supper and they were splendid. From there we ran to Cypress
Harbour where we anchored for the night. A fellow anchored
close to us had been trolling for cohoes. They are getting

5½ cents a pound for their fish. He had made $10 today. We passed quite a number of trollers round Wells Pass and Sutlej Channel.

(August 27, 1934)

Already, at Drury Inlet, the *Toketie* had begun her southward run, homeward bound. The days grew ever shorter and the evening mists crept round earlier. *Toketie* made an occasional stop on the journey south, dodging the first winds of autumn. Re-entering the Strait of Georgia, she left the land of the dark cedars in her wake and felt the warm September wind blowing from the yellowed coast.

One year the Barrows greeted old friends at Pender Harbour before crossing to the Ballenas Islands, just north of Nanaimo Harbour.

> Tied up to the mooring in the bay N.W. of the Ballenas lighthouse. We had lunch as soon as we arrived, which Amy had been cooking on our way across the strait, a delicious mutton stew, part of the ingredients given us by our kind friends in Pender Harbour. They also provided us with the stewed apple which followed. After lunch I went ashore. Mr. and Mrs. Dane, the light-keepers, gave me a hearty welcome and showed me the light and house and I took a photo of them and the lighthouse. Dane was an engineer on the *Black Raven* at one time, as well as the *Columbia,* and knew many of our friends further up the coast. They came back to *Toketie* and we showed them the photos and had a yarn. Now we know that the bay we were in, and the next little bay, are quite useful places in a south-easter.

(September 8, 1935)

According to an article written by Bea Hamilton in 1966, in the First World War Doug Dane went from England to India to Vladivostok and across Siberia to Perm, then returned to England by way of Siberia, the Pacific Ocean, North America and the Atlantic Ocean. After discharge he came to British Columbia. While engineer aboard the mission ship *Columbia,* he met Bessie, who was then hospital matron at Pender Harbour. They spent a year at the Sisters Light Station off Lasqueti Island, where there was not a scrap of vegetation, before being transferred to Ballenas Island, which Bessie called "a paradise compared to the Sisters".[7] Desiring a cow on their little island, they bought a freshened heifer named Scotty which was brought by the ship *Estevan* and unceremoniously dumped into the sea about a quarter of a mile off shore. Perhaps it was Bessie's loud calls of "Come Scotty" that guided the floundering cow to a good feed of oats on shore. When the Second World War began, Bessie went to work as Y.M.C.A. War Service Supervisor, responsible for social and recreational activities at Esquimalt and Naden. Doug was made a Chief Petty Officer in the navy. After the war he became engineer on *M.V. Cy Peck,* serving the Gulf Islands. Bessie and Doug settled down at Fulford Harbour, on Salt Spring Island.

Entering Nanaimo Harbour, the *Toketie* was back in familiar waters.

> Splendid weather with a light S. to S.W. breeze. On arriving at Nanaimo we tied alongside the *Atrivida,* and Tom came on board and saw the photos I had taken on the trip. We moved to Anderson's Boathouse and then went to the barber's and got our hairs cut. After which we had supper at the Malaspina Hotel. The dogs had a feed of bones, and we took them for a walk before returning to *Toketie.*
>
> (September 12, 1933)

> Cowie skimmed the engine valves and ground them, and by 6.30 P.M. the engine was ready to run again. I was glad I had them attended to, as there was a good deal of carbon under some of them after a cruise of over 1100 miles.
>
> (September 13, 1933)

> Tom Higgs paid us a visit. He said there was another petroglyph at Jack Point, further along towards Jarrett's and we decided to run over in the afternoon. Tom came along about 3 P.M. and we johnsoned over to Jack Point. We could not find the petroglyph but Tom is getting further data. We went up to the Plaza for supper and had a fried sole each. They were so big that they stalled us.
>
> (September 9, 1935)

The Barrows were fond of Tom Higgs, whose father, Leonard Higgs, was a nephew of Arthur Reed Spalding of Pender Island. In 1886 young Leonard Higgs came to live near his uncle, and there young Tom grew up, living what seems an idyllic life: helping on his father's farm, visiting friends on the nearby islands, hunting, fishing, and playing grass hockey, cricket and poker. In 1931, only two years before the Barrow summer journals begin, Tom and his brother William had a small motor ferry (50 tons weight, about 66 feet long) built at New Westminster, for the Higgs Gabriola Ferry Company Ltd. The new ferry was named *Atrevida* after the Spanish corvette whose captain had discovered Gabriola Island only 140 years earlier; it was one of the two vessels of Malaspina's expedition of 1791 which had anchored at the very spot where the new ferry docked on its daily runs to Gabriola Island. Five years after the *Atrevida's* first run, Tom Higgs had three boats working in Nanaimo Harbour.

> We left Nanaimo and ran as far as Percy Anchorage as the tide was flooding rather strong in Dodd's Narrows. We made fast to the wharf and talked to the miners who were trolling, but at the moment were waiting for high tide to start fishing. They were fishing commercially, selling all the salmon at Nanaimo and giving coal-mining a rest. We were amused at the performances of an old hayseed skipper with a tug and a big scow. He had never been to False Narrows and wanted to get to the brickyard. He had no chart or tide-table.
>
> (September 3, 1936)

The Gabriola Brick Yard was located almost at False Narrows, a perilously shallow passage choked with rocks and dangerous indeed for a tug and scow.

> We ran to Thetis Island and anchored by the dophins at the booming ground. Amy rowed us over to the Fraines and we saw Mrs. F. and a friend who was stopping with them. After lunch we took *Toketie* over and made fast to their spar buoy. They all came on board and had a chat. We said good-bye and returned to the booming ground. We then johnsoned over to the Booth's and had supper with them, and talked over the events of the summer. It was a beautiful night.
>
> (September 4, 1938)

> Retreat Cove, Galiano Island. We got a warm welcome from the Simpsons. They showed us their garden which is as good as could be, the growth of cabbages and cauliflowers etc. being remarkable. After supper we talked till ten o'clock when we re-

turned to *Toketie* which brought to a close a happy anniversary
of our wedding day.

As we approach the waters adjacent to our home
I think it only fitting to write just one more pome,
The theme of which, I'm sure you'll guess, & needless
    to relate
Concerns the lid, of squarehead style, A. wears upon
    her pate.
It's been stepped upon & sat upon, but comes up for
    more & more
Yet looks as chic & stylish as in good old days of yore.
But one thing is quite certain, that how oft we go to
    sea,
It will stand up to our cruises, as well as *Toketie.*
                     (September 20, 1941)

The Simpsons invited us to a delicious chicken dinner at noon.
Afterwards I took a few movies of the mallard ducks and the
dogs. In the afternoon the Simpsons and Alfie came out to the
launch, and we had hardly got aboard when Cyril and K. Morgan
were seen up at the house. Alfie went ashore for them and
brought them out to *Toketie* and we all had tea on board. The
Simpsons with their usual generosity gave us walnuts, apples,
quinces, and vegetables to take away with us.
                     (September 21, 1941)

Ran to the Stanier's. We showed Doc the photos and the Cine
camera and stayed to lunch, moving homewards at 3.20. Thus
ended our summer cruise, which was a sad one for us. No
longer can we be known up the coast as the people in the small
boat with the two black dogs, for dear old Nannie has gone to
the place where all dogs and humans must eventually go, and
we are left with many memories of our constant companion of
many years, and her dear little ways.
                     (September 4, 1936)

Nanette's death at Cracroft Island was omitted, to avoid the con-
fusion of the subsequent references to her in this account, which
telescopes all the voyages into one long trip.

Amy was up with Nannie during the night. There is a sick cat
on one of the gillnet boats and Mrs. Gillnetter said she was giv-

ing it olive oil and OXO, the same treatment Amy is giving
Nannie, only she is using Mineral Oil.

(August 7, 1936)

Our dear little Nannie passed away this morning in Amy's lap
and we miss her dreadfully. Later on we buried her at sea, on
which our two little dogs and ourselves have passed so many
happy days for many years past. She was everybody's friend, but
just devoted to Amy, and Amy to her.

(August 9, 1936)

Leaving the Staniers, the *Toketie* at last reached the home dock at
North Saanich.

After two hours we arrived home, our long cruise ended. We
renewed old acquaintances, and met new friends, and nobody
took a shotgun to us, so that I presume they were pleased to see
us, as we were certainly pleased to see them.

(September 16, 1938)

CHAPTER SEVEN

Since the Gulf Islands are his own backyard, Francis Barrow does not write of them in his sea journals of the Thirties. For him, a departure is from Nanaimo. A glimpse of the southern islands must be drawn from the early journals of 1903 and 1905, brief though these entries are, and from Barrow's letters to his friends Harlan Smith and Billy Newcombe.

Francis was 27 years old when he arrived in British Columbia to visit his brother. In that year, his earliest surviving journal records a rowing holiday and gives some glimpses of island life just after the turn of the century.

> Left Victoria 7 A.M. for Sidney. Got there at 8 & met Arthur. We went on board *S.S. Iroquois* and got to Mayne Island about 12 o'clock. We left there in a row boat with camping outfit etc.

for N. Pender I. Lovely day and most enjoyable trip. Camped near Postmaster's house, a man named Auchterlonie.

(April 1, 1903)

Although the Gulf Islands were discovered by Spanish and British explorers in the 1790s, it was 1850 or later before settlers came to Salt Spring, Galiano, Mayne, Saturna and the Pender Islands. Some of these first islanders were from England, from the same social class as the Barrows; on their island homesteads they used calling cards, gave formal dinners, and played tennis, field hockey and cricket, a style of living frequently made possible by "remittances" of income from England. They also farmed. Many of the remittance men were younger sons of wealthy families, sent to the colonies to learn farming and be "landed gentry". Released from the rigidity of British society, keen on hunting, fishing, sports and adventure, they lived with good humour, excellent manners and physical endurance. Their era was short-lived, for many died in the First World War.

Those living on the Gulf Islands had good service from the *S.S. Iroquois* to keep them in touch with each other and with the larger world, or a strong arm at the oars brought them to Sidney where they could get a train to Victoria. Although the dry forests of these islands were easily penetrated and homesteaders could visit each other on foot, the sea was their highway and everyone had boats. From the moment of his arrival on the British Columbia coast, Francis Barrow is concerned with the sea. His later travels up coast are only an extension of his daily environment.

Pender Island. Got up at 6.30 and spent morning sizing up the country. Arthur and I got away with 18 eggs in two meals besides other things. Eggs 20 cents a dozen. Left about 3 o'clock. Camped for the night at head of Browning Harbour.

(April 2, 1903)

When Francis and Arthur Barrow arrived at Hope Bay on Pender Island on that April afternoon, they were only 16 years behind Noah Buckley and David Hope, the two men who had originally pre-empted this part of the island in 1887. When David Hope died, leaving his share of the land to his brother and sister in Scotland, his brother-in-law Lawrence Auchterlonie made the long journey across an ocean and a continent to inspect the inheritance. His glowing reports quickly brought out the rest of the family. He soon turned over management of the back-breaking farm to his son James, the first postmaster and later justice of the peace. Elderly Lawrence Auchterlonie was living in a cabin nearby at the time of the Barrow brothers' camping trip. At first James raised sheep and hogs, growing a few acres of peas for the hogs, seeding the land down to clover and grass for hay and pasture. Gradually the fields, hard-won from the forest, became richer and he was able to buy Jersey cows. However, time would reveal that the land base of the islands could not sustain farming on a large scale and most of these early farms did not survive. Sheep proved to be the enduring crop of the island farmer.

> After breakfast had a jaw with two brothers of the name of Hamilton. Left Browning Harbour 12.30 for S. Pender I. Went through canal and arrived at Stanford's place. He was away but we broke into his house and made ourselves pretty comfortable. At supper we finished our 50th egg. All day long we heard the blue grouse drumming in the woods and all night long the frogs kept on croaking.
>
> (April 3, 1903)

The Hamilton brothers were also from Scotland. The elder brother, Alexander, came as a stonecutter from Carluke to the stone-yard of Mr. John Mortimer in Victoria. Sent to Pender Island to quarry stone at Browning Harbour, Alexander was so enchanted with the lovely crescent beach at the head of the harbour that he promptly pre-empted a quarter section, built a log cabin and began clearing land. In 1888 he returned to Scotland to fetch his bride, Jeannie Leiper, and his younger brother Hugh. Perhaps they told the Barrows of the work in dredging the canal, for the Barrows must have been among the first travellers to take advantage of this short cut between Browning Harbour and Bedwell Harbour.

It is not too surprising that Arthur Stanford was not at home when the Barrow brothers came to his door. He is typical of the "remittance men", who were so numerous before the First World War. A son of the English publishing family, with an excellent library in his log cabin, Stanford ran sheep, poultry and hogs on his farm at Camp Bay (later the Craddock estate). Mrs. Freeman of Pender Island has remarked that raising hogs was "hardly compatible with his way of life, for when city lights beckoned, it was root hog or die."[1] At one time he also had a cow, but the poor beast broke her leg wandering amidst the logs and had to be shot. Faced with the problem of utilizing the dead cow, this ingenious young man lit a fire under his wash boiler, cut the cow into small pieces and boiled the beef into a meat essence, like Oxo. This he cut into cubes which he wrapped in greased paper and sold to his grocer in Victoria. From the familiar way the Barrow brothers moved into Stanford's house, it may be assumed that they were old friends, perhaps from schooldays in England.

Slacked about all day; read Stanford's books. Egg total 77. People on the Islands manage to kindle fires in a first class way. Pitch wood is pretty common and it is only necessary to cut a few shavings off a piece of pitch wood and these will kindle any fire. A particular kind of fir tree also grows on most of the islands with a thick bark on it. The tree is ringed with an ax, a couple of auger holes bored in it & a fire is lighted in one of the holes, the other hole about 1½″ being put in at an angle to the first one (about 2″ in diameter) so as to make a draught. The bark breaks off when the tree falls down.

(April 4, 1903)

Left S. Pender 12 o'clock & got to Bedwell Harbour 1 P.M. Moresby Island 3.30, where we stayed. We had the wind against us all the way & a pretty choppy sea crossing from Bedwell Harbour to Moresby Id. I felt rather rotten & Arthur said I looked like a piece of old pork. It was pretty hard work rowing for Arthur, so after rowing away from Moresby for 2 hours on our way to Sidney we went ashore on an unknown island on which we had seen a house, with the intention of making a camp there. We found the house with three young ladies in charge, the owner of the island being away. We had just put things in shape about camp & were going off to the wharf to pull up the boat when we encountered the owner of the island who wanted to know who we were & where we had got our boat as it belonged to him. We told him & after a few explanations got on friendly terms. After helping him unload his stink-boat we went back to camp & turned in for the night. Egg total 90.

(April 5, 1903)

Went to lunch with the islanders, Mrs. Rant (who arrived in the stink-boat), 3 daughters, & the boss of the island, one Mair. Strong wind blowing so could not make Sidney as we had intended. Turned in early. Good lot of rain during night. Had a big fire in front of the tent so things were pretty snug.

(April 6, 1903)

Left for Sidney at 7 P.M. where we arrived at 9.15. Could not get any grub at hotel so Arthur walked back to Victoria. I put up at Hotel Sidney, not being able to walk 16 miles without any dinner. Egg total up to 7 P.M. since April 1st (evening) about 104.

(April 7, 1903)

Blown ashore by an April storm, Francis Barrow was introduced to Mr. Mair and Hill Island (the "unknown island" of his diary), where in 1905 he established a camp and, not surprisingly, a poultry farm. Diary entries now noted the building of coops and runs and the numbers of eggs, chickens and ducks. At the bottom of each page he tallied the buckets of water carried against the number of eggs produced. There were continual boat breakdowns and repairs, a subject of concern throughout his life.

In November 1903 an entry announced: "Got my ticket for the Old Country" and ten days later "took the engine out of my boat and put it in the barn and cleaned it". On November 28 in Victoria, "paid bills and saw about getting my dogs looked after, etc." He crossed Canada by train and at Montreal boarded the *Bavarian* for England. On this return to England, Barrow almost certainly courted Amy Bradford, who was half-sister to his brother Arthur's wife Daisy, but the Scribbling Diary of 1905 only reveals that he is back in North Saanich.

Came out to Sidney on the morning train. Parson Payne and Baker on train. They wanted to go to Saturna, but *Iroquois* did not let out. I took them in the launch. Stopped at Hill Id. for grub. Stopped S. end of Moresby Id. for a time – too much wind. Went on round N. end of Pender and then on to Saturna. Stayed night at the Parson's.

(April 1, 1905)

This entry may record the first of many shared sea experiences with the famous Payne family of Saturna Island. Members of the third generation of Paynes in Canada, Dorothy Richardson, Geral-

dine Hulbert and Dora Payne, have given an excellent description
of this family, an example of the compromises made by English settlers between the old life in England and the new Canadian style.
Gerald arrived first, aged 16, in 1886, and lived for six years on War-
burton Pike's ranch before pre-empting 900 acres for himself on Saturna Island. His brother Harold bought land in Winter Cove, Saturna Island, and soon two other brothers came, Hubert and
Charles, and two sisters, Katie Bradley-Dyne and Isobel. The Reverend Hubert Payne, Harold's twin, lived at Winter Cove also; at the
water's edge, with the help of his brother-in-law Major Bradley-
Dyne, he rebuilt a Japanese boat-house into a tiny church named
St. Christopher's. Many boats would be tied to the little dock on a
Sunday morning while their owners crowded into the chapel to
share the service conducted by Hubert Payne. Hubert was less
sanctimonious in his ex-naval pinnace, *Gazelle,* and islanders were
accustomed to seeing the boat drifting helplessly, with Parson
Payne's head occasionally emerging to shout "Confound the thing!"
or worse, "JERUSALEM!".

In August 1905, Barrow's diary recorded preparations for another
trip to England, and in September 1906, he and Amy Bradford were
married, coming immediately to honeymoon on Saturna Island,
where Amy was introduced to the Payne family. On December 10
of the same year, Francis bought the North Saanich Hotel near Sidney, and this historic old building became their first home.

The North Saanich Hotel was built by Henry Brackman, a cabin
boy on the sailing ships who abandoned sea life to seek gold in the
Cariboo. Coming out of the Gold Rush with $40,000 to invest, he
met a man named Milne, who knew about manufacturing oatmeal
and who helped Brackman establish a mill near Sidney. In 1883
Brackman was joined by young David Ker who had learned the
milling business in San Francisco. The Brackman-Ker enterprise
expanded, building a long wharf that stretched 150 feet into Tse-
hum Harbour (now Shoal Bay). When the water supply on the four-
acre property proved inadequate, the business was moved to Victoria and the Saanich mill was converted to a hotel, store and post
office run by Mr. and Mrs. Alex Wright. Arthur and Francis Barrow
were frequent guests at the hotel. Wright's death in 1903 and Henry
Brackman's in 1906 led to the decision to sell, and Barrow was able
to buy it all for $3,250 with ten dollars down, the price including all
the hotel furnishings. The general store and post office, which had

served Gulf Islanders as well as the North Saanich people, was moved to Sidney.

In 1914 the war began and Francis Barrow returned to England with the rest of his friends, but apparently his physical condition relegated him to non-combatant duties. He was back in British Columbia in 1916. A photograph album shows farming work and tennis parties, and the *Toketie* log lists departures and arrivals. Geraldine (Payne) Hulbert records a cruise, when she was 13, in the Gerry Payne vessel *Irene*, with the *Truant* belonging to a Mr. Adams, the *Toketie* with the Barrows aboard, and Uncle Harold Payne in the *Varuna*. "On calm days we would all tie up together – they weren't very large boats – in one of the inlets."[2]

1931 is the date of the first of many letters to Newcombe, the anthropologist:

> We were up at Saturna Island a little while ago and we saw Jerry Payne and his family on the *Irene*. Jerry wanted us to go and see an Indian sitting in his grave at Monarch Head. The bank had got washed down by the sea and left him exposed. We did not have time, but I said we would be blowing in at Boot Bay with you before long and Jerry was pleased to hear we were coming.

The early letters begin "My dear Newcombe" but soon the more familiar "Dear Billy" is used. At this time Barrow was also corresponding with Harlan Smith, the first Canadian rock-art specialist; in a letter dated November 6, 1933, Barrow banters:

> My dear Newcombe, I think it is up to you to provide me with a stenographer to cope with my Harlan Smith correspondence, since you were responsible for starting it. A few days ago I got a six page letter which was continued on four or five more pages. Some of the letter I will have to get you to make clear to me sometime, but I have answered it. I got about 20 geological maps of the coast from the dear old man also, which are very nice. Also rafts of typewritten sheets on various subjects. He told me he had your letter, and he seems ready to get busy on a monograph dealing with the Petroglyphs and Pictographs of the Province. I told him I would be pleased to contribute $50 towards the cost of publication. I believe the typesetting, if Harlan Smith's article is printed in the American Anthropol-

ogist, is free, but illustrations are not. It is well to have as many
illustrations as possible, don't you think?

The following letter of April 7, 1934, written from the *Toketie* anchored at Arrowhead Beach near Swartz Bay on the Saanich Peninsula, conveys the warmth of the friendship and a picture of some
Barrow activities.

My dear Newcombe, Pray pardon a pencil note, but there will
be hell to pay if I do not send you a report of our doings. We
left home on Wednesday about 8 P.M. and ran to Montague
Harbour [Galiano Island] where we roosted for the night near
our old time artifact hunting ground. Thursday about 2 P.M.
Jackson drove us to the Morgan's where we left a sack of seed
potatoes and in exchange they gave us a fine ham just out of the
smokehouse. Later they drove us to the Burrills', Fred and Joe
very well and in good form. Fred's rock garden is a joy to see as
is also the Morgan's. A session of cribbage with Morgans
finished up the day and we walked back to *Toketie* through the
silent woods and turned in about midnight. Dick insisted on
my having one of his labrets, the one you saw which he found
in Active Pass near the Georgeson place. He has another of the
top hat shape, a little battered. I did not like to take the labret,
but Dick seemed to wish me to do so, so I am going to give him
a lock-up case for his collection, which is getting to be quite a
nice little one. Nigel, Morgan's eldest son, a young fellow of
about 20, is a keen birds egg collector & he told me of the spots
where gulls nested locally & I have passed on the information
to Munro. Yesterday morning Nigel came down to the boat,
and we went to Twin Ids, just N.W. of Wise Id. There were a
considerable number of gulls about, and on the two small islets
a dozen or more nests nearly completed of newly gathered
grass and feathers. Pretty early for April 6th. Nigel is going to
let Munro know if he sees any of the Corge cormorants
nesting. We are having a lovely lunch: beef pie & purple top
broccoli, cold, with dressing & jelly gravy, rhubarb, coffee. No
cover charges. In the meantime the tide is going down, which
will admit of us getting some clams to fish for sole with, & also
to give the beach by the log dump the once over lower down
than last time. We will be home in a day or two. I have not

sown any garden yet, but this lovely weather is too good to miss. The locker lids are fine. Amy thanks you very much and says she has utmost peace. One lid fell down & took the skin off my fingers but that was not your fault.

Frequently named in the letters is their good friend Cyril Morgan, at one time a collector of taxes on Galiano Island and resident there for close to 40 years. On the occasion described in this letter, Francis also visited the Burrill brothers, Joe and Fred. Joseph Burrill left his home, a quiet Yorkshire vicarage, in 1893, finally finding Galiano Island in 1896, where he bought 80 acres of the sun-warmed southeast corner of the island. Three years later his older brother Fred came to run the farm and do the cooking and gardening. Mary Kingsmill has written of their store where you went not only to shop but "to spend an hour or so chatting". Both the store and the tradition survive today. In the early years the Burrills made grocery deliveries with oxen, but they later acquired Ben, a horse with a mind of his own. Joe Burrill would of course stop for tea and gossip when he made his deliveries, but if he stayed too long, Ben would depart for home, and Mr. Burrill would have to walk the long miles back, to begin his delivery route once more. Ben "was retired at a ripe age and lived in comfort for years even though the Burrills had to rise early and hoist his rheumatic old bones up with a block and tackle each morning."[3]

These are some of the friends of the Barrows' island community, to whom they returned each autumn. With photographs, note-books and memories of the upcoast summer, the Barrows would settle into the activities of a raincoast winter on the Saanich Peninsula. Barrow reported to Harlan Smith:

I have been busy making a water-wheel for a friend on Galiano Id. to furnish power to charge his radio battery, and Newcombe and I went up last week to put it in place. The dam gave trouble so we could not see it running. Since our return I have been plumbing and painting. We have enlarged the kitchen and put in a new sink and I had to alter water pipes and drain, pipe-fitting being one of my pleasures.

Smith replied:

It must be wonderful to live where you do, where it is quiet, with nice air to breathe and enjoy an out-of-doors' life, with annual trips on the salt chuck. Perhaps some day I may have the pleasure of trying my hand at such activities as dam-building, pipe-fitting etc. in British Columbia... you may be thankful that you lead a civilized life."

"'Chuck' is Chinook jargon for 'water' and when you're on it you'll find a paradox around every headland and a tale in every harbour", Gilean Douglas has remarked.[4]

Harlan Smith was one of Canada's first archaeologists. In 1911 he was given the post of archaeologist in the newly formed Division of Anthropology of the Geological Survey of Canada, devoting the rest of his career (26 years) to the collection of Canadian anthropological data. He had been a member of the famous Jessup North Pacific Expedition to Washington, British Columbia, Alaska and northeast Russia, organized by the American Museum of Natural History, which amassed the data which has made the northwest coast one of the most thoroughly documented areas of the world, anthropologically speaking. Encouraging Francis Barrow's work, Smith wrote, "I consider your [rock-art recording] work to be thorough, and so exact and truthful that it would be acceptable in the very best archaeological and anthropological publications".[5]

In a letter to Harlan Smith, Francis expressed his grief over the loss of the beloved cocker spaniels, first Nanette, then Rinnie.

> I had a great sorrow last Wednesday. My little dog was run over by a car just outside our house and instantly killed. So now our two spaniels who have grown old with us have gone within six weeks.

After 1941 the letters more frequently refer to ill health, for Francis seemed increasingly susceptible to colds and Amy suffered from arthritis and neuritis. The cruise of 1941 was the last of those upcoast expeditions. In 1942 Barrow wrote to Billy Newcombe:

> Last Thursday evening I showed last year's cruise film at a meeting of the Masons at Saanichton, after they had held a conference. They all stood up after we had had coffee & sandwiches and cake & I stood up too. My old friend Tom Walker of Brentwood started speaking, and I found that he was saying a lot of very nice things about me, and I sat down feeling rather over-

come by his kind remarks. I am not accustomed to having kind things said about me in public.

In June of the same year, Barrow wrote concerning an article he had written for the *Canadian Geographical Journal,* to Newcombe:

Just a few lines to advise you of the packet I have left. It is a follow-up to my article in the February [1942] number of the *Canadian Geographical Journal.* I wonder if you would be so very kind as to look it over. I got $40 for the article and they seemed pleased with it. Percy Belsen, in a Canadian Forestry Corps in the north of Scotland, broke his ankle, and while in hospital there saw the number in the hospital reading room. He was so pleased to see something so near to his home that he read it twice ... I felt when I wrote these little articles what a very great debt of gratitude I owe you, for all that I have learned in the field of archaeology is due entirely to you, and I should have liked to have said so.

In 1944, only two years after the writing of this letter, Francis Barrow was dead, after catching a cold and a chill. He left his books to his brother Arthur, of Johnson's Landing in the Kootenays, and the beloved boat *Toketie* was willed to Joseph John. A document dated December 12, 1944, records that for $310 the executors of the estate of Francis John Barrow transferred 64 shares in the vessel to Amy, who apparently wanted to hold on to the boat she also loved. At some later date Amy returned those shares to their close young friend, Joe John. Old *Toketie,* now owned by marine architect William Garden, is still in use, mainly ferrying passengers from Toad Landing to Canoe Cove.

Amy Barrow lived on, in increasing pain from arthritis, for 18 years after Francis' death. She remained in the house at Toketie Point until she was too crippled to take care of herself. She died in a nursing home, with May John's arms around her. Amy Barrow left an estate of $300,000 to two nephews, two nieces and a step-nephew. Earlier, the house at Toketie Point had been sold to Joe and May John. No stone marks the graves of Amy and Francis Barrow, for both ordered that their ashes be scattered at Toketie Point.

How well the Barrows loved this island world with its raging tide rips and snug anchorages, and its amazing variety of people. How

Francis Barrow savoured the food he ate and how patiently he studied the idiosyncrasies of *Toketie*'s motor. The Barrows are gone. But perhaps their gentle lives can serve some further purpose if this retelling of their friendly voyaging re-awakens forgotten memories, stirs to life old laughter, tells children or grandchildren or great-grandchildren something of the lives from which they descend. Perhaps others, following in the wake of the *Toketie*, can glimpse the ghosts of the upcoast people with whom the Barrows were always ready to share a yarn or a game of crib.

FOOTNOTES

CHAPTER ONE

1. Bonella Woodhead. Letters to the author.

2. Sarah Mallet. Undated unpublished reminiscences in the possession of May John, Sidney, B.C.

CHAPTER TWO

1. Bessie Dane. Interview with the author.

2. Jackie Holecka. "Pender Harbour: a Steamer Stop", in *Raincoast Chronicles* v.1, n.1, 1972, p.31.

3. Will Dawson. *Ahoy There*. Toronto and Vancouver, J. M. Dent, 1955, p.174.

4. Bessie Dane. Interview with the author.

5. Gilean Douglas. "He Sowed by the Waters", in *Family Herald and Weekly Star*, June 21, 1951, p.34.

6. Ella M. Mason. *Lasqueti Island, History and Memory*. South Wellington, B.C., Self-published, 1976, p.71.

7. Bessie Dane. Interview with the author.

CHAPTER THREE

1. Moira Farrow. "The Skipper and the House of a Million Words", in *The Vancouver Sun*, September 20, 1973, p.41.

2. Frank H. Ellis. "The Deer of Hardy Island", in *The Daily Colonist*, June 4, 1972, p.6.

3. Maggie Leach. "Inlet Offers Magnificent Scenery", in *The Columbian*, February 26, 1927, p.8.

4. Howard White. "They don't make 'em anymore: Peck Easthope", in *Raincoast Chronicles First Five*. Madeira Park, Harbour Publishing, 1976, p.256.

5. Stephen E. Hilson. *Exploring Puget Sound and British Columbia*. Holland, Michigan, Van Winkle Publishing Company, 1975, p.62.

CHAPTER FOUR

1. Archibald Menzies. *Menzies' Journal of Vancouver's Voyage April to October, 1792*. Archives of British Columbia Memoir No.5, Victoria, 1923, p.76.

2. Howard White and Jim Spilsbury. "Q.C.A. The Accidental Airline", in *Raincoast Chronicles 9* Madeira Park, Raincoast Historical Society, no date, p.49.

3. Francis Barrow to Harlan Smith. Letter, May 10, 1934.

4. T. W. Paterson. "British Columbia Characters", in *Canada West Magazine*, v.7, n.2, 1971, p.31.

5. N. S. Strickland. "Echo of Pioneers", in *The Vancouver Province*, December 28, 1974, p.28.

6. Ibid.

7. Ibid.

8. Will Dawson. "Delightful Desolation", manuscript in the Provincial Archives of British Columbia, no date.

9. James Stirrat Marshall and Carrie Marshall. *Vancouver's Voyage*. Vancouver, Mitchell Press Ltd., 1955, p.41.

10. Archibald Menzies. Op. cit.

11. Gilean Douglas. *The Protected Place*. Sidney, Gray's Publishing Ltd., 1979, p. 60.

12. W. B. Woodward. "Cortes Pioneer Crosses the Bar", in *The Vancouver Sun*, October 16, 1948.

13. Ruth McVeigh. "Quadra resident writes and reflects", in *The Campbell River Courier*, May 10, 1974, p.6.

14. Doris Andersen. *Evergreen Islands*. Sidney, Gray's Publishing Ltd., 1979, p.58.

CHAPTER FIVE

1. Union Steamship Company. *Annual Report, 1926*.

2. Peter Chapman. *Navigating the Coast: a History of the Union Steamship Company*. Sound Heritage, v.6, n.2. Victoria, Provincial Archives of British Columbia, 1977, p.33.

3. *Sailing Directions, British Columbia Coast (South Portion)*.v.1, 8th ed. Victoria, Department of the Environment, 1973, p.241.

4. Joe Gregson. "Pioneer Joe Gregson's own story", in *The Fisherman*, December 3, 1971, p.5.

5. Ibid.

6. *British Columbia Archaeological and Historical Sites Protection Act*, 1960.

7. Frank Morris and W. R. Heath. *Marine Atlas of the Northwest*. Seattle, P.B.I. Company, no date, p.35.

8. Edith Bendickson. "Mission Ship Always Welcome", in *The Daily Colonist*, March 21, 1976, p. 14.

CHAPTER SIX

1. Leslie Peterson. "Her medal caps a life at the top", in *The Vancouver Sun*, February 14, 1973, p.73.

2. Beth Day. *Grizzlies in their Backyard.* New York, Messner, 1956, p.15.

3. "Finds old friend dead after long journey", in *Nanaimo Free Press*, May 14, 1955, p.1.

4. Doras Kirk. "Plunder and Desecration", in *The Daily Colonist*, June 23, 1974, p.8.

5. Stephen E. Hilson. *Exploring Puget Sound and British Columbia.* Holland, Michigan, Van Winkle Publishing Company, 1975, p.88.

6. Frank Morris and W. R. Heath. *Marine Atlas of the Northwest.* Seattle, P.B.I. Company, no date, p. 42.

7. Bea Hamilton. "Mighty Glad to Retire on Salt Spring", in *Victoria Daily Colonist*, January 23, 1966, p.11.

CHAPTER SEVEN

1. B. J. Spalding Freeman. "South Pender Island", in *A Gulf Islands Patchwork.* Sidney, Peninsula Printing Company Ltd., 1961, p. 171.

2. Derek Reimer, ed. *The Gulf Islanders.* Sound Heritage, v.5, n.4. Victoria, Provincial Archives of British Columbia, 1976, p.58.

3. Mary Kingsmill. "Some Impressions of Galiano", in *A Gulf Islands Patchwork.* Sidney, Peninsula Printing Company Ltd., 1961, p.154.

4. Gilean Douglas. "Salt-Chuck Salvation", in *British Columbia, a Centennial Anthology.* R. E. Watters, ed. Toronto, McClelland and Stewart, 1958, p.214.

5. Harlan Smith to Francis Barrow. Letter, June 14, 1935.

SOURCES

Books and Pamphlets

Pamela Amoss. *Coast Salish Spirit Dancing.* Seattle, University of Seattle Press, 1978.

Doris Andersen. *Evergreen Islands.* Sidney, Gray's Publishing Ltd., 1979.

Muriel Blanchet. *The Curve of Time.* Sidney, Gray's Publishing Ltd., 1977.

British Columbia Archaeological and Historical Sites Protection Act, 1960.

Bruce Calhoun. *Northwest Passages.* San Francisco, Miller Freeman Publications, 1971.

———— and James F. Macdonald. *Mac and the Princess.* Seattle, Ricwalt Publishing Company, 1976.

Peter Chapman. *Navigating the Coast: a History of the Union Steamship Company.* Sound Heritage, v.6, n.2. Victoria, Provincial Archives of British Columbia, 1977.

Michael Coney. *Forest Ranger, Ahoy!.* Sidney, Porthole Press Ltd., 1983.

Margaret Craven. *I Heard the Owl Call my Name.* London, Pan Books, 1974.

Will Dawson. *Ahoy There.* Toronto and Vancouver, J. M. Dent, 1955.

Beth Day. *Grizzlies in their Backyard.* New York, Messner, 1956. (Reprinted as *World of the Grizzlies.* New York, Doubleday, 1969.)

Gilean Douglas. *The Protected Place.* Sidney, Gray's Publishing Ltd., 1979.

Frances Duncan. *The Sayward-Kelsey Bay Saga.* Courtenay, Argus Press, 1958.

Ed Gould. *Logging.* Saanichton, Hancock House, 1975.

Gulf Islands Branch, British Columbia Historical Association. *A Gulf Islands Patchwork.* Sidney, Peninsula Printing Company Ltd., 1961.

William Halliday. *Potlatch and Totem.* London, J. M. Dent, 1935.

Beth Hill. *Indian Petroglyphs of the Pacific Northwest.* Saanichton, Hancock House, 1974.

Stephen E. Hilson. *Exploring Puget Sound and British Columbia.* Holland, Michigan, Van Winkle Publishing Company, 1975.

James Stirrat Marshall and Carrie Marshall. *Vancouver's Voyage.* Vancouver, Mitchell Press Ltd., 1955.

Ella M. Mason. *Lasqueti Island, History and Memory.* South Wellington, B.C., self-published, 1976.

Archibald Menzies. *Menzies' Journal of Vancouver's Voyage April to October, 1792.* Archives of British Columbia Memoir No.5, Victoria, 1923.

Milestone 1958. Elphinstone Junior-Senior High School Yearbook, Gibsons, B.C.

Frank Morris and W. R. Heath. *Marine Atlas of the Northwest.* Seattle, P.B.I. Company, no date.

Don Munday. *The Unknown Mountain.* London, Hodder and Stoughton, 1948.

Phyllis and Don Munday. *Wild Flowers of British Columbia.* Vancouver, Mitchell Press, 1958.

Derek Reimer, ed. *The Gulf Islanders.* Sound Heritage, v.5, n.4., Victoria, Provincial Archives of British Columbia, 1976.

Harry Roberts. *Trail of the Chack Chack.* New York, Carlton Press, 1968.

Roberts Creek Historical Committee. *Remembering Roberts Creek.* Madeira Park, Harbour Publishing, 1978.

G. A. Rushton. *Whistle up the Inlet.* Vancouver, J. J. Douglas, 1974.

Sailing Directions, British Columbia Coast (South Portion). v.1, 8th ed. Victoria, Department of the Environment, 1973.

Published Articles

"Adventurous Couple Collect Indian Signs on B.C. Coast", in *The Vancouver Sun*, September 14, 1934.

Francis J. Barrow. "Petroglyphs and pictographs on the British Columbia Coast", in *Canadian Geographical Journal*, v.24, n.2, February 1942.

Edith Bendickson. "Mission Ship Always Welcome", in *The Daily Colonist*, March 21, 1976.

"Brackman-Ker Milling Co. Celebrates Golden Jubilee of Successful Enterprise", in *The Daily Colonist*, June 24, 1928.

Don Bunyan. "Harlan I. Smith, Pioneer Contributor to Western Archaeology", in *The Midden*, v.11, n.3, 1979.

Alfred Carmichael. "Coast Journey Goes Beyond Mere Drive", "Pulp History Launched at Alberni", and "Troubles Beset Pulp Makers", in *The Daily Colonist Magazine*, September 23, October 2, and October 9, 1955.

Cecil Clark. "Jim Stanton", in *The Daily Colonist*, February 25, March 1, and March 4, 1962.

"Cortes Pioneer Passes", in *The Daily Colonist*, January 16, 1956.

Emily A. Courtwright. "Timber down the Hill", in *Datum*, v.6, n.4, 1981.

J. H. Dawson. "Many Struggles Marked Initial Construction", in *Powell River News*, January Progress Edition, 1949.

Will Dawson. "Pender Harbour", in *The Vancouver Sun*, April 15, 1950.

————. "Surprise Island", in *The Province B.C. Magazine*, March 30, 1957.

"Death of Dean Brock Closes Brilliant Career", in *The Vancouver Province*, July 31, 1935.

Charles M. Defieux. "Letters Clear up Mystery of Old Ship's Figurehead", in *The Vancouver Sun*, May 15, 1965.

Francis Dickie. "New log transporter carries own cranes", in *The Daily Colonist*, June 6, 1965.

Gilean Douglas. "He Sowed by the Waters", in *Family Herald and Weekly Star*, June 21, 1951.

————. "Kingcome Kingdom", in *The Daily Colonist*, October 13, 1951.

————. "Salt-Chuck Salvation", in *British Columbia, a Centennial Anthology*. R. E. Watters, ed. Toronto, McClelland and Stewart, 1958.

————. "Sailor for Christ", in *The Daily Colonist*, September 5, 1965.

————. "The Bible Barge to Kingdom Come", in *Raincoast Chronicles 10*. Madeira Park, Raincoast Historical Society, no date.

Frank H. Ellis. "The Deer of Hardy Island", in *The Daily Colonist*, June 4, 1972.

Moira Farrow. "The Skipper and the House of a Million Words", in *The Vancouver Sun*, September 20, 1973.

"Finds old friend dead after long journey", in *Nanaimo Free Press*, May 14, 1955.

Joe Gregson. "Pioneer Joe Gregson's own story", in *The Fisherman*, December 3, 1971.

Bea Hamilton. "Mighty Glad to Retire on Salt Spring", in *Victoria Daily Colonist*, January 23, 1966.

Lyn Hancock. "Skipper Chack Chack of Nelson Island", in *The Daily Colonist*, February 2, 1975.

Bill Heybroek. "Bones Bay Cannery", in *The Daily Colonist*, January 12, 1975.

Jackie Holecka. "Pender Harbour: a Steamer Stop", in *Raincoast Chronicles*, v.1, n.1, 1972.

Bert Hudson. "Victoria's Gentle Servant of the Arts", in *The Daily Colonist*, September 6, 1964.

"Indian Authority", in *The Victoria Times*, March 28, 1944.

Doras Kirk. "Plunder and Desecration", in *The Daily Colonist*, June 23, 1974.

Bill Law. "Old Timer only took Union Fish", in *The Fisherman*, September 11, 1964.

Scott Lawrance. "Eulachon Salvation", in *Raincoast Chronicles First Five*. Madeira Park, Harbour Publishing, 1976.

Maggie Leach. "Inlet Offers Magnificent Scenery", in *The Columbian*, February 26, 1927.

B. A. McKelvie. "Great Totem at Kingcome Inlet has Welcomed Many", in *The Vancouver Province*, October 18, 1927.

A. McKenzie. "Shirt-sleeved Tycoons", in *The Vancouver Province*, December 27, 1947.

Ruth McVeigh. "Quadra resident writes and reflects", in *The Campbell River Courier*, May 10, 1974.

George Nicholson. "Theirs the Wilderness", in *The Daily Colonist*, August 30, 1959.

"The Old Man of Gorge Harbour", in *The Daily Colonist*, August 1, 1948.

T. W. Paterson. "British Columbia Characters", in *Canada West Magazine*, v.7, n.2, 1971.

Leslie Peterson. "Her medal caps a life at the top", in *The Vancouver Sun*, February 14, 1973.

Lester R. Peterson. "British Columbia's Depopulated Coast", in *Raincoast Chronicles First Five*. Madeira Park, Harbour Publishing, 1976.

"Pioneer dies", in *The Province*, March 5, 1935.

"$301,060 left by Pioneer", in *The Daily Colonist*, January 5, 1963.

Peg Pyner. "Uncle John Manson laid to rest on Cortes", in *The Campbell River Courier*, January 23, 1957.

John A. Radford. "Happy Summer Days at the Yuclataws", in *The Vancouver Sun*, 1934.

"Ran Gabriola Ferry for Years", in *The Nanaimo Daily Free Press*, March 15, 1960.

"Resident of Sidney", in *The Daily Colonist*, March 28, 1944.

Violet Seaman. "Texada Lime", in *Powell River News*, October 8, 1947.

Neville Shanks. "Barran Quit Flying for Table Tennis", in *The Daily Colonist*, August 11, 1974.

N. S. Strickland. "Echo of Pioneers", in *The Vancouver Province*, December 28, 1974.

Peter Trower. "From the Hill to the Spill: (A breathless history of B.C. logging)", in *Raincoast Chronicles First Five*. Madeira Park, Harbour Publishing, 1976.

"Henry Twidle dies, age 77", in *The Campbell River Courier*, April 4, 1956.

Jean Wallbank. "Life on Harbledown Island", in *The Daily Colonist*, July 13, 1975.

Howard White. "They don't make 'em anymore: Peck Easthope", in *Raincoast Chronicles First Five*. Madeira Park, Harbour Publishing, 1976.

———— and Jim Spilsbury. "Q.C.A. The Accidental Airline", in *Raincoast Chronicles 9*, Madeira Park, Raincoast Historical Society, no date.

W. B. Woodward. "Cortes Pioneer Crosses the Bar", in *The Vancouver Sun*, October 16, 1948.

Unpublished Articles

Will Dawson. "Delightful Desolation". Manuscript in Provincial Archives of British Columbia, no date.

Doris Lundy. "The Rock Art of the Northwest Coast". M.A. thesis, Simon Fraser University, 1969.

Sarah Mallet. Reminiscences in the possession of May John, Sidney, B.C., no date.

Lester Peterson. "Report to the National Museum of Canada concerning rock paintings of the Jervis Inlet area". Ottawa, National Museum of Canada, 1966.

Correspondence

William Newcombe/Francis Barrow correspondence. Provincial Archives of British Columbia, Victoria.

Harlan Smith/Francis Barrow correspondence. National Museum of Canada, Ottawa.

Index